5 33

D1299984

Growth, Shortage and Efficiency

Yrjö Waldemar Jahnsson, 1877–1936, was Professor of Economics at the Institute of Technology, Helsinki. In 1954, his wife Hilma Jahnsson established, in accordance with her husband's wishes, a foundation.
The specific purpose of the Yrjö Jahnsson Foundation is to promote economic research in Finland. To this end the Foundation supports the work of individual scholars and institutions by awarding them scholarships and grants. It also invites internationally renowned economists to Finland to give courses of lectures which are then published in this series.

YRJÖ JAHNSSON LECTURES

Kenneth J. Arrow
Aspects of the Theory of Risk-Bearing

Assar Lindbeck
Monetary-Fiscal Analysis and General Equilibrium

L. R. Klein
An Essay on the Theory of Economic Prediction

Harry G. Johnson
The Two-Sector Model of General Equilibrium

John Hicks
The Crisis in Keynesian Economics

E. Malinvaud
The Theory of Unemployment Reconsidered

James Tobin
Asset Accumulation and Economic Activity

YRJÖ JAHNSSON LECTURES

Growth, Shortage and Efficiency

A Macrodynamic Model of the Socialist Economy

JÁNOS KORNAI

Translated by Ilona Lukács

UNIVERSITY OF CALIFORNIA PRESS
Berkeley and Los Angeles

WITHDRAWN ITHACA COLLEGE LIBRARY

University of California Press
Berkeley and Los Angeles, California

Copyright © The Yrjö Jahnsson Foundation 1982

Library of Congress Catalog Card Number : 82-51121
ISBN 0-520-04901-2

Printed in the United States of America

0 1 2 3 4 5 6 7 8 9

Contents

Foreword

I consider it a great honour to have been asked to deliver the Jahnsson lectures of 1980. I feel indebted to the Yrjö Jahnsson Foundation for having given me impulse to think over once more the problems that were to be treated in the lectures. My hosts – first of all Professor J. Paunio and Dr S. Honkapohja – did their best to make the discussions following my lectures as fruitful for me as possible.

As a 'rehearsal' for the Jahnsson lectures, a favourable opportunity was offered by the invitation from the Institute of Economics of the Catholic University of Louvain, Louvain-la-Neuve. May I take this opportunity to thank Professors J. Drèze, P. Mándy and H. Tulkens as well as the other Belgian colleagues for their valuable remarks.

I am particularly grateful to András Simonovits, who assisted me in clarifying a few mathematical problems treated in this text. Some results of our research, related to the topics of my Jahnsson lectures but not discussed in detail in the present book, will be published in the near future (jointly with András Simonovits).

Zsuzsa Kapitány helped me with the computer programming of the simulation exercises; Péter Wellisch with the clarification of mathematical–statistical problems as well as with computations; Attila Chikán, Mrs Z. Halmi, Mária Lackó, Ede Lovas, Márta Nagy and Péter Pete with data collection. Although I shall refer to their work in appropriate places later on, I also wish to thank them now for their valuable assistance.

Several of my colleagues read the manuscript: some have already been mentioned, but I shall now add the names of Zsuzsa Dániel, János Gács and Béla Martos. I feel grateful for their useful advice.

Finally, I wish to express my gratitude to the translator, Ilona Lukács, and to the language editor, Dr Paul Hare, for their devoted work.

János Kornai
Budapest

1
Introduction

This study is centred on a *growth model* designed to represent and analyse some properties of the socialist economic system. Long-term growth is now an unfashionable subject. However, I think it is high time at least some economists turned their attention to the imperishable issues of growth.

The literature on the theory of growth has become enormous. Instead of supplying a long list I shall only mention three names, of those whose influence on the present study is the most tangible. These are *von Neumann*, *Harrod* and *Kalecki*.[1] It was not my aim to create something new and original from the growth-theoretical point of view. On the contrary, I shall be quite content if, in the present work, the reader recognizes a few theorems which he has already learnt well in another context. I shall try to establish a connection between the theory of growth according to Neumann–Harrod–Kalecki on the one hand, and my own ideas concerning the socialist economy on the other.

[1] In Hungary several important research works have been completed in recent years on the subject of applying growth theory to the analysis of a socialist economy. I should mention in particular the works of M. Augusztinovics and her fellow researchers; I. Ligeti; J. Rimler; J. Sivák; Gy. Szakolczai and his team; as well as Gy. Szepesi and B. Székely.

The present study is an organic continuation of my previous works. *Anti-Equilibrium* set forth a few ideas concerning the *general methodological foundations* underlying the theoretical examination of economic systems. My book *Economics of Shortage* sought to contribute to the *microeconomic* theory of the socialist economy. The volume *Non-Price Control* – edited together with Béla Martos – discussed the scope for the application of *mathematical control theory*, and in particular, of a special form of regulation, called *control by norms*.[2]

The present study complements these works by contributing to the *dynamic macrotheory* of the socialist economy. Of course, just as for those earlier works, this one is also far from exhausting its subject; instead, it merely outlines a few thoughts.

I have tried to arrange this study in such a way that it can also be understood by those who may not be acquainted with my earlier works. Yet I am afraid that I only half-succeeded. Limited space has sometimes forced me to 'settle' in just a few words certain difficult questions that required entire chapters in my earlier writings. I am not sure whether I can succeed in convincing the reader of the correctness of the approach used in my study; and, even if I may hope to achieve that, I can expect it mainly

---

[2] J. Kornai, *Anti-Equilibrium*, North-Holland, Amsterdam, 1971; J. Kornai, *Economics of Shortage*, North-Holland, Amsterdam, 1980; J. Kornai and B. Martos (eds), *Non-Price Control*, North-Holland and the Publishing House of the Hungarian Academy of Sciences, Amsterdam and Budapest, 1981.

A simulation study based on Hungarian data and carried out by a team under the guidance of the author using a macroeconometric dynamic model can also be considered as a further preliminary of the present research. J. Gács, Zs. Kapitány and M. Lackó contributed to this work. Several unpublished papers were written about the model and computations carried out with it.

from those readers who are familiar with the other books mentioned below, and who understand the connections between the ideas raised here and the theoretical and methodological foundations explained earlier.[3]

This book is mainly concerned with the description of the growth model, and the economic interpretation of its assumptions and conclusions. I do not go into the mathematical analysis of the model, into the mathematical proofs of the propositions, or into formal–technical questions; these are left for other publications.

Finally, one more remark. The 'main product' of the present work is the attempt to apply growth theory in the investigation of certain problems of the *socialist* economy. At the same time, I would like to see a few 'by-products' as well, such as observations on *general* methodological principles, which would also prove useful in the examination of other socioeconomic systems.

[3] For those who do not intend to read the books mentioned above, but who would not shrink from a shorter reading list, may I recommend as an introduction, the article 'Resource-constrained versus demand-constrained systems', *Econometrica*, 47 (1979), 801–20. The present book can also be interpreted as a transformation of the 'visual' hydrodynamic model ('reservoirs', 'pumps', 'taps', etc.), described in the article, into a *mathematical* model.

Reading of the article may be supplemented by looking through Chapters 9–14 and 20 of *Economics of Shortage*.

2
Main Characteristics of the Model

Main properties

The most characteristic features of the model are the following:

(I) We describe a *dynamic* system. In mathematical terms, the model is represented by a system of difference-equations.

With the aid of the model we shall describe both *long-term* and *short-term* processes and shall examine their interactions.

Both *stock* and *flow* variables appear in the model, linked by dynamic balance equations. In consistently applying the stock–flow approach we deviate from a number of other growth-theoretical models, for example from most applications of the Neumann model and of the dynamic Leontief models.[1]

(II) In its aggregate form the model describes the *real sphere*: production, investment, trade and consumption. At the same time it describes, endogenously, the *control sphere* which guides the real sphere. In other words, it represents by equations the behaviour of decision-makers.

---

[1] On the significance of the stock–flow approach, important ideas are raised in the paper by J. C. Schoenman: 'The Crisis in Equilibrium Economics' (manuscript), 1978–79.

This is again a deviation from the bulk of the growth-theoretical literature which confines itself to the examination of the real sphere.

(III) In describing the real sphere we apply several different simplifying assumptions, yet these are not bound up with the particularities of the socialist economy. For better or worse, the growth of the real sphere of any economic system can be described using this particular block of the model. In contrast to this, *the description of the control sphere is system-specific*. It is set up in order to capture certain attributes of the control mechanisms of the Eastern European socialist countries. Without repeatedly referring to this during the discussion, I shall always keep in view an economy that functions within the social relations and institutional framework of today's Eastern-European socialist countries.

The model does not reflect the particular features of Hungarian economic control as it developed following the reform of 1968. Instead, it tries to describe the traditional, pre-reform mechanism of Eastern European economies, and, in addition, the common properties of the pre-reform and post-reform economic administration.

(IV) The analysis is not normative; I have no intention of making recommendations on economic policy. We shall try to understand – to describe and to explain – a few properties of the growth of the socialist economy. Economic policy is not considered as something existing outside the system and controlling it from there – listening to economists' recommendations, following the advice of normative models, or personal judgement. *Economic policy is an endogenous part of the system*.[2] Even though

---

[2] I have borrowed this expression from Assar Lindbeck. (See 'Stabilization policy in open economies with endogenous politicians', *American Economic Review*, 66 (1976), Papers and Proceedings, 1–19.)

in an immensely simplified form, the model tries to reflect the reactions and behavioural regularities of the economic policy-maker and of the planner.

(V) This is a study in *pure theory*. Numbers only appear in the text sporadically, and exclusively for illustrative purposes.

The model described in detail in the next chapter is not intended to serve as a macroeconometric model; we do not plan to estimate the parameters, and to do quantitative analysis. Instead, what we want to achieve with the present model is merely a number of *qualitative* propositions.

I foster the hope that at some time in the future my work may serve as a starting-point for macroeconometric studies. If that should happen, the model will obviously have to be transformed in two respects. First: actual analysis of the economic history of the country concerned would probably make it clear that further variables and equations need to be incorporated, certain relationships will have to be modified, the lag structure of the model transformed, and so on. On the plane of pure theory a much greater degree of simplification is possible and necessary than that acceptable in a statistically based econometric model.

Second: in the case of macroeconometric application, the definitions of variables and parameters and, along with them, the structure of equations would have to be adjusted to suit the available data. This kind of adaptation inevitably entails a lot of concessions which have to be granted for the sake of quantification. However, this is not necessary as yet. In the present case the theory has been formulated first, to be followed – encouraged by the demands of theory, or, reformulating theory in the light of practical measurement difficulties – by the methodology of measurement.

(VI) The structure of the model is unsuitable for representing endogenously the *transitions* from one historical period to the next. It is intended to clarify how growth and its control take place under *'ordinary'* or *'normal' conditions*, within a stable institutional system and under more or less stable external conditions.

General assumptions

For the construction of the model we shall employ several assumptions. The most broadly general ones are mentioned in advance, and the rest are treated in the course of the discussion.

General assumption 1. The economy is examined at the national *macro*-level. No breakdown by industries is introduced.

General assumption 2. The economy contains two sectors with distinct social roles: the state- and co-operative-owned *firms' sector*, and the *household sector*. The facts that there exist in the Eastern-European socialist countries privately owned firms, and further, that there exist informal and unofficial types of private activity, the so-called 'second economy', are disregarded. Non-profit institutions functioning with a legal status different from that of firms are also disregarded. The state budget does not appear explicitly, either on the side of revenues or on that of expenditures. What is called the 'government sector' in many Western macromodels appears only partly in our model, in the form of the public firms' sector.

The inclusion of additional sectors in the model does not seem impossible: this could be done at a later stage of the research work. At this point, however, when the initial steps are being taken, it would unnecessarily encumber the pure theoretical approach. The sector of public firms comprises an overwhelming proportion of production activity, which is the most characteristic feature of a socialist economy. Accordingly, it will be useful to focus our attention on this sector.

Socialist firms are, in reality, governed by a multi-level control mechanism. In our severely aggregated model we cannot go into the details of the influence of each management level separately, nor into their interactions. The equations describing the control of the firms' sector are designed to represent the joint outcome of the activities of the upper-, medium- and lower-level managers and planners, and of the central and the firms' decision-makers.

General assumption 3. We are describing a *closed* economy: we disregard foreign trade and international financial and credit linkages. This is, of course, a very strong simplification. Most of the Eastern-European socialist countries, including Hungary, have an open economy. As with the previous assumption, 'to open up' the model would not entail insoluble difficulties in constructing the model. In a later phase of the research work, and particularly when it comes to macroeconometric application, it would be worth attempting it. Yet I chose not to do it in the present, initial phase of the work, for it would render an already large equation system even more complicated. Besides, I wish to illuminate those problems which arise in a socialist economy *from within* rather than those caused by external linkages. From this standpoint, it is particularly advantageous if, as the first stage of theoretical research, we investigate a closed economy.

General assumption 4. In this model *money* does not appear. As contrasted with those above, I do not feel that this assumption is very strong, but rather a justified approximation to reality in describing the given institutional system.

Let us take first the firms' sector. It is clear that in the traditional form of the socialist economy – that is even before the decentralizing reform – financial accounting of the firm's trade transactions takes place. Despite that, this sphere is only monetized in appearance. The budget constraint of the firm is rather 'soft': its decision-makers are only loosely bound by it. As a rule, it is not a binding constraint; it does not restrain the firm's freedom of choice. Money thus plays a passive role. The money supply available for firms is adjusted basically to money demand; that is, in the final account, to the spending possibilities consistent with the given real resources. Financing is adjusted to the real transfers, and accordingly, saving is adjusted to real investment.[3]

General assumption 4 would obviously be unjustified in modelling a market economy in which each important sector, including therefore the firms' sector, faces a hard budget constraint. In our case, however, this assumption is not only permissible for the sake of simplification, but it is also necessary, in order to give a realistic description of the firm's behaviour and of the control of production.

In the household sector the budget constraint is hard; it effectively restrains household decisions about consumption. But even the household considers real rather than nominal income when deciding on its spending or saving. Therefore, as a first approximation, it seems appropriate for the effects of nominal income and the consumer price level on household behaviour to be considered together. Consequently, only real income and real consumption of the household should be included in our model.[4]

[3] The Hungarian reform of economic management introduced in 1968 increased the role of money but, at least up to the end of 1979 when the research work underlying the present model was finished, it had not led to any genuine 'hard' budget constraint, or really active money in the firms' sector.
[4] The separation of nominal incomes and the consumer price level would not lead to serious difficulties in the equations of the model that describe the behaviour of households. *This* separation is neglected in fact only for the sake of simplification.

General assumption 5. We deal exclusively with *storable products* and disregard services (except labour).

General assumption 6. Labour is the only primary resource. The role of natural resources is disregarded.

Any relaxation of general assumptions 5 and 6 would substantially alter the mathematical nature of our model and make formal analysis difficult. Thus, for the time being, we must insist on these simplifications. This leads us to the last assumption.

General assumption 7. In the model there are no inequalities, upper or lower bounds. Apart from one bilinear relationship, the equations are linear.

I apply general assumption 7 reluctantly. It is only accepted here to ensure that the resulting mathematical model should be tractable. It would be desirable to replace it, as soon as possible, by a formulation somewhat closer to reality.

3
The Variables and Equations

In the following we shall examine in turn the model's variables and equations. In my view, at the present stage of the research it is *the model itself* that should be regarded as the main result of the work accomplished so far, much more so than the analysis based on it. Above all, I wish to demonstrate that *there exists a relatively simple formalism, which can be used to describe certain regularities of growth, and its self-regulation in a socialist economy.*

Appendix A lists the variables and parameters alphabetically, and the equations are presented in a definite sequence (to be explained later). Here in Chapter 3 we shall survey the variables and equations, classifying them into categories different from those of the Appendix. The sequence is now adjusted to the logic of economic exposition and clarification.

Shortage

The phenomenon of shortage plays a central role in our train of thought. Although the model analyses the national economy at the *macro*-level, we must set out from the *micro*economic foundations in order to deal with shortage.

Let us consider a single elementary purchasing action of a buyer: at a given time he wishes to acquire a given product. The well-known relationship is as follows:

$$\begin{matrix} \text{demand} & - & \text{actual purchase} \\ \text{(ex-ante} & & \text{(ex-post} \\ \text{variable)} & & \text{variable)} \end{matrix} \left\{ \begin{matrix} = 0, & \text{purchase intention} \\ & \text{fulfilled} \\ > 0, & \text{excess demand.} \end{matrix} \right.$$

Standard microeconomics usually stops at this point. And yet it is worth asking the question: what happens if the initial demand is left unsatisfied?

The buyer effectuates *forced adjustment* in various alternative forms. He substitutes another product – more expensive or of a poorer quality – for the one originally desired; that is he accomplishes *forced substitution*. If the desired product is not available promptly, but only through *queuing*, the buyer may join the queue. He may try *search*: visiting various shops, trying to find the desired goods. Or the purchase may be *postponed* to a later time.

In my own 'vocabulary' shortage is a category comprising a large group of phenomena. It includes not only the divergence between purchasing intention and realization ('excess demand'), but also the various forms of forced adjustment. The shortage syndrome is experienced by households living in a chronic-shortage economy. And it is also felt constantly by firms, both in the process of acquiring material inputs, and in their utilization in the course of production.

'Shortage' is a summary expression referring to numerous elementary shortage events. Its measurement involves particular difficulties. It cannot be done by straightforward summation, since it is obvious that we cannot directly add up the indicators of events and processes that are qualitatively totally different. Therefore, if we wish to represent shortage phenomena within a macromodel, we must use some indirect methods of measurement.

The first task is to assemble a large number of *partial shortage indicators*. Let them be denoted by $z_1(t)$, $z_2(t)$, ..., $z_n(t)$. Each partial shortage indicator measures the intensity of certain definite shortage phenomena in a particular field (for example residential construction, pharmaceutical production, food purchase). Some examples: the share of forced substitution in total pur-purchases or in total consumption; the number of those queuing up or the queuing time; the number of selling establishments visited or the search time; the number of orders refused; time lost in production due to the shortage of inputs; and so on.

In the present study, concerned with the formulation of a theoretical model, it is sufficient to observe that *a comprehensive and regular observation of partial shortage indicators is possible*. There is no theoretical or methodo-logical obstacle to the organization of such observation. (It is another question that in the statistical practice of socialist countries such indicators are only sporadically observed, so that only very few long time series are avail-able for us.)[1]

All partial shortage indicators are measured in their own units. Only two general properties are stipulated in defining them.

(i) Higher values of any partial shortage indicator show more intensive shortage, while lower values show less intensive shortage.

---

[1] Table B.1 in Appendix B presents two examples of partial shortage indicators based on Hungarian data: the time-series of queuing for private cars, and that of orders refused by the building industry.

(ii) Each partial shortage indicator is non-negative. It assumes the value zero if the process reflected by the indicator is in a *Walrasian state* – that is to say, when it does not show any shortage phenomena. For example when the share of forced substitution is zero; the number of queuers is zero; waiting time in production caused by input shortage is zero, etc. For some partial shortage indicators there is a natural zero point, but for others there remains a certain arbitrariness.

Let us assume that we have to hand a large number of partial shortage indicators; a collection suitably reflecting a representative sample of the millions of different shortage phenomena. The number of these representative partial shortage indicators is n. Now comes the second task, that of building up from them a *synthetic* index. Let us denote the *macroindex of shortage intensity* by $\bar{Z}(t)$.

$$\bar{Z}(t) = \phi(z_1(t), \quad z_2(t), \ldots, z_n(t)). \quad (3.1)$$

The function ϕ is constructed in such a way as to have the following properties:

(1) The function ϕ is increasing in all its arguments. If, therefore, the values of all partial shortage indicators are unchanged, except for one that has increased, the intensity of shortage at the macro-level also increases.

(2) The macroindex $\bar{Z}(t)$ is a non-negative variable. It takes the value zero in the Walrasian state:

$$\bar{Z}(t) = 0 \Leftrightarrow z_1(t) = 0, z_2(t) = 0, \ldots, z_n(t) = 0. \quad (3.2)$$

Thus the index $\bar{Z}(t)$ can be regarded as *a potential measure of the distance from the Walrasian state*, provided that it satisfies some further requirements not discussed here.

(3) The unit of measurement for the index $\bar{Z}(t)$ can be arbitrary; that is, it is determined up to a multiplication by a positive constant.[2]

(4) The index $\bar{Z}(t)$ *should reflect the positively corre-lated motion over time of the various partial shortage indi-cators.* Accordingly, the selection of the function ϕ involves specifying an *appropriate mathematical–statistical proce-dure,* capable of representing the positively correlated motion of the various partial shortage indicators $z_i(t)$.

In a real economic system the partial shortage indicators are not, of course, perfectly correlated but there are several circumstances that create quite a strong positive correlation between them.

(*a*) In the case of shortage, an individual decision-maker can, as I have mentioned, choose among various possibilities for action: he can effectuate forced substitution, or post-pone purchase, or search for the desired product, etc. How-ever, for the set of decision-makers as a whole, on a given market or in a given producing sector, the different alterna-tive actions are distributed in definite proportions. These distributions are more or less unchanged over time. Accord-

---

[2] Stipulation (ii) concerning the partial indicators and stipulation (2) concerning the macroindex – the latter determining the locus of the origin – are desirable from the point of view of *certain theoretical analyses* undertaken in the present study. (For an example, see Figure 6, below.) As opposed to this, the locus of the origin is irrele-vant from the point of view of the *growth model* described in the remainder of this chapter. Therefore, we could allow the index $\bar{Z}(t)$ to be determined not only up to a multiplication by a positive con-stant, but a constant could also be added to it.

ingly, if shortage is generally intensifying, there will be more forced substitutions, *and* more postponements, *and* more search, etc.

(*b*) Of course, the intensity of shortage does not grow or decline uniformly in the market for each product or in each field of utilization. The queue of purchasers for cars may grow, while the housing shortage may ease, or the other way round. Yet in the chronic-shortage economy a certain equalizing tendency is present. Shortage serves also as a *signal* in the different allocation mechanisms. The intensification of shortage in certain fields has the consequence that, sooner or later, resources will be redirected there from other fields where shortage phenomena are not so distressing.

(*c*) There also exist causal relations between different shortage phenomena. If there is a shortage of some input at one point of production, it will, as a rule, hold up the output, which may in turn cause a new form of shortage where the output is used, and so on. Shortage spills over in this way from one area to another.

For all these reasons it is reasonable to expect that positive correlation between different shortage indicators should be considerable. Besides, in determining the instantaneous intensity of each concrete shortage phenomenon a role is also played by different specific factors. The macro-index $\bar{Z}(t)$ is designed to reflect the common and general factors leading to similar movements in the various partial indicators, neglecting the specific factors leading to divergent movements.[3]

---

[3] Within the economy a *deliberate reallocation of shortage* may take place. For example, shortage intensity in domestic consumption may be reduced if economic policy redirects the burdens of shortage to investment – or conversely. With systematic negative correlations the

The magnitude of the macroindex $\bar{Z}(t)$ is undoubtedly influenced by the kinds of partial indicators $z_i(t)$ and the type of function ϕ (that is the type of mathematical-statistical procedure) being used. This arbitrariness is, however, more of a *technical* character and primarily reflects the difficulties of determining suitable indicators and selecting the statistical procedure. The macroindex $\bar{Z}(t)$ is designed to reflect, more or less accurately, the *objectively* existing joint motion of *objectively* existing and observable partial phenomena, and not a subjective value-judgement about the difficulties or losses caused by shortage.

The index $\bar{Z}(t)$ is a *latent variable* of the system.[4] The latent variable describes an essential, overall property of a system in quantitative form. It is 'latent', in that it is not directly observable: its magnitude can only be determined

---

use of more than one macroindex may be useful. For example, $\bar{Z}^{cons}(t)$ would be the macroindex of shortage in consumption, $\bar{Z}^{inv}(t)$ the macroindex of shortage in investment, etc.

The question of 'one macroindex or more' goes beyond the scope of the present study, though it would be worth clarifying in the framework of a macroeconometric analysis. In the present book it is assumed all along that positive correlations among the partial shortage indicators are substantial, so that the general shortage situation in the system is satisfactorily measurable by a single synthetic shortage index.

[4] The distinguished Swedish statistician and economist Hermann Wold drew my attention, during a personal conversation, to the possibility that statistical methodology concerned with latent variables might be the most appropriate approach to the synthetic measurement of shortage. I wish to take this opportunity to thank him for the help he gave me, through this suggestion as well as through several of his studies. (See for example 'Model Construction and Evaluation when Theoretical Knowledge is Scarce' (mimeo-

in an indirect way, by inference from the analysis of other observed ('manifest') indicators. The measurement of latent variables was first undertaken by psychometry and sociometry. (E.g. human 'ability' or 'talent' is such a latent variable. It is not directly measurable, yet one can draw conclusions about its magnitude from several actually measurable properties or performances.) The problem already has an extensive mathematical–statistical literature, and econometric applications are becoming more widespread.[5]

We shall make a short detour here and try to clarify the relation of our shortage macroindex to the category of 'aggregate excess demand' well known from macroeconomics. They are clearly related to each other in content, for both seek to express the general degree of shortage at the macro-level. At the same time, there are important differences.

One important difference is that aggregate excess demand only captures one (though very important) aspect of shortage: the purchase intention frustrated because of shortage. As opposed to this, the index $\bar{Z}(t)$ comprises the multitudinous components of shortage phenomena, including the various forms of forced adjustment.

There is another important difference between the two

---

graphed), Faculté des Sciences Economiques et Sociales, Université de Genève, 1979.)

I am also grateful to the Swedish economist A. Markowski who drew my attention in a similar direction.

[5] See for example H. M. Blalock (ed.), *Measurement in the Social Sciences*, Macmillan, London, 1974; D. J. Aigner and A. S. Goldberger (eds), *Latent Variables in Socio-Economic Models*, North-Holland, Amsterdam, 1977.

From the Hungarian literature we shall mention the works of Gy. Meszéna, J. Rimler and M. Ziermann.

categories. The definition of aggregate excess demand is as follows: the sum of individual excess demands minus the sum of individual excess supplies. This is, therefore, the net balance of deviations in both directions from the Walrasian balance. As contrasted with this, our index $\bar{Z}(t)$ reflects only the shortage side, without deducing surpluses from it. In a chronic-shortage economy (what is more, in every economy, at least to some extent), shortage and slack coexist. 'Netting out', that is the subtraction of excess supplies from excess demands, obscures some real problems of the economy.[6]

In Appendix C we present a small computation, in which the value of the macroindex $\bar{Z}(t)$ was determined for the years 1968–78 from Hungarian data, using principal component analysis. I should emphasize that the computation is offered only for illustration. We do not claim that principal component analysis is the only or even the best means of operationalizing the function ϕ. We only sought to demonstrate that the techniques of multivariate statistical analysis do make it possible to determine our macroindex $\bar{Z}(t)$.

At this point I shall break off the discussion of the question, aware that several problems have been left unsolved. Some of them belong to the sphere of the general theory of economic measurement, others are of an econometric-statistical character. Further research work is necessary. It may yet turn out that the ideas as outlined above – as well as the properties specified for the variables $z_i(t)$ and $\bar{Z}(t)$, etc. – need to be amended in several respects. In any case,

[6] Obviously one may construct another macroindex which would – analogously with the index $\bar{Z}(t)$ – reflect slack in a synthetic form: the under-utilization of fixed capital and other resources. This may be done later when elaborating the further developed versions of the model.

consideration of this sphere of problems suggests that *it is possible to develop a macroindex which reflects syntheti-cally the intensity of shortage*. And this is enough for us to make progress in the present study in constructing a dynamic macromodel of the shortage economy.

The macroindex of shortage appears as an *explanatory variable* in numerous equations of the model. It plays a two-fold role.

In one part of the equation system shortage appears as a *signal* or, in other words, as an *information variable*, to which the firms' sector or the household sector react through their decisions. In this way the perception of shortage operates in the control sphere.

In another part of the equation system shortage appears as a *real variable*, influencing the efficiency of production and investment. In that part, shortage directly affects the real sphere.

After briefly explaining the roles to be played by the macroindex of shortage as an explanatory variable in different equations, we now shift to the other side and consider the equation that explains, within our model, the motion of the variable $\bar{Z}(t)$ itself. Let us assume for a moment that the economy is more or less stationary; the volume of production, even though fluctuating, has a constant mean over an extended period. The equation explaining shortage in this case then takes the following form:

$$
\begin{aligned}
\bar{Z}(t) = \bar{Z}^*(t) &+ \zeta_K(K(t) - K^*(t)) \\
&- \zeta_U(U(t) - U^*(t)) \\
&- \zeta_V(V(t) - V^*(t)) \\
&+ \zeta_Z(\bar{Z}(t-1) - \bar{Z}^*(t-1)).
\end{aligned}
\tag{3.3}
$$

On the right hand side of the equation the first term is $\bar{Z}^*(t)$, the normal intensity of shortage, briefly: *normal shortage*. Our assumption is the following:

$$\bar{Z}^*(t) = \bar{Z}^* = \text{constant.} \qquad (3.4)$$

This is one of the basic assumptions in the model. In reality, the normal degree of shortage may shift over a long period: it may decrease or increase. Later on we shall revert to this question. At this point, however, we can express our assumption thus: *for a given economic system, in a definite historical period characterized by more or less stable institutional conditions, normal shortage is given and unchanged over time.*[7] It is not the task of our model to explain why exactly $\bar{Z}$ is the normal shortage, and why it is not more or not less. This would only be revealed by other studies based on an analysis of the history, social conditions and institutional framework of the economy in question. Equation (3.3) is designed solely to clarify why the actual intensity of shortage in year t deviates from normal. I feel that this may, though strictly delimited, be an important and fruitful way of putting the question. Numerous branches of science – such as biology, medicine, social psychology, technical science – often put their questions in a similar form and arrive at remarkably interesting answers. According to equation (3.3), actual shortage is more intensive than normal,

---

[7] The category of *normality* plays a central role in our train of thought. We shall not offer a detailed explanation immediately; instead its interpretation evolves gradually in the course of the study. For a more detailed explanation see the earlier works mentioned in footnote 2 of Chapter 1.

(*a*) if the investment process is over-ambitious, or, if the actual investment commitment[8] of the national economy, $K(t)$ exceeds the normal commitment $K^*(t)$;

(*b*) if the actual output stock: $U(t)$, or the actual input stock: $V(t)$ is smaller than the normal stock: $U^*(t)$, or $V^*(t)$ respectively, and therefore the buyer or the producer experience greater difficulty in finding the desired goods or the input needed for production;

(*c*) if the previous year's shortage was more intensive than normal, and this has worsened the present year's shortage. That means that the last term represents an auto-regressive effect: the temporal spill-over of the consequences of shortage.

We cannot claim that the equation includes all the explanatory variables that might be relevant, but it does draw attention to a few of the most important ones.

The coefficients express the *'strength' of the reaction* to deviations from the normal state. Similar parameters appear in a number of other equations, but we shall not give any further explanation. (A list of these can be found in Appendix A.)

Let us now revert to our temporary assumption concerning the stationary character of the economy. Of course, the assumption cannot be maintained, since it is precisely the growth of the economy that is the subject of our examination. Yet relaxing it leads to a formal-

---

[8] In describing the model, we are compelled to introduce the variables in a 'successive manner'. In the equations presented earlier certain variables appear that can only be explained later. This is what happens now, for example, with the variables $K(t)$, $U(t)$ and $V(t)$. At this point we can only throw light on their economic content through a brief reference.

methodological difficulty. For let us suppose now that the variables representing production, investment and consumption are growing over time, while the index $\bar{Z}(t)$ fluctuates around its own constant normal value. This would not cause any difficulty if, for example, we had assumed a multiplicative form of relationship between the shortage index and the real stock or real flow variables. Unfortunately, in accordance with general assumption 7, we must insist on linear forms for mathematical convenience. However, in such circumstances the magnitude of the shortage variable will tend to lag, as time passes, increasingly behind the magnitude of the real variables. In order to circumvent the resulting difficulties, we shall resort to a technical 'trick'. We shall 'scale up' the index $\bar{Z}(t)$ by a growth factor denoted by Γ_Z:

$$Z(t) = \Gamma_Z^t \bar{Z}(t), \ \Gamma_Z > 1. \tag{3.5}$$

(The superfix, t, denotes Γ_Z raised to the tth power.)

In accordance with this, we modify the original assumption concerning the constancy over time of normal shortage. Formula (3.4) is therefore replaced by the following:[9]

$$Z^*(t) = \Gamma_Z^t \ Z_0^*, \tag{3.6°}$$

in which

$$Z_0^* = \bar{Z}^* = \bar{Z}^*(0). \tag{3.7}$$

---

[9] The symbol ° added to the equation number identifies those formulae that form part of the model's final system of equations.

Finally, equation (3.3) explaining actual shortage is replaced – using relationships (3.5) and (3.6°) – by the following equation:

$$
\begin{aligned}
Z(t) = Z^*(t) &+ \zeta_K(K(t) - K^*(t)) \\
&- \zeta_U(U(t) - U^*(t)) \\
&- \zeta_V(V(t) - V^*(t)) \\
&+ \zeta_Z(Z(t - 1) - Z^*(t - 1)).
\end{aligned}
\tag{3.8°}
$$

In the ensuing discussion the original actual shortage macroindex $\bar{Z}(t)$ and the original normal shortage $\bar{Z}^*$ are no longer used; instead, $Z(t)$ and $Z^*(t)$ (without a bar) scaled up according to (3.5) and (3.6°) will appear. I wish, however, to emphasize once again that this is merely a technical trick used for the sake of linearity, and it does not change essentially the economic interpretation of these variables.

Household demand and purchases

The demand of the household sector depends on a number of explanatory factors: consumer prices, past and present nominal incomes, the accumulated wealth of the household, expectations concerning the future, etc. Let us consider all these factors as given and constant, so that we can express household demand as a function of a single explanatory variable, namely shortage. We are examining a given year t, so that the argument referring to time can be omitted.

Let us denote the *demand* of the household sector by

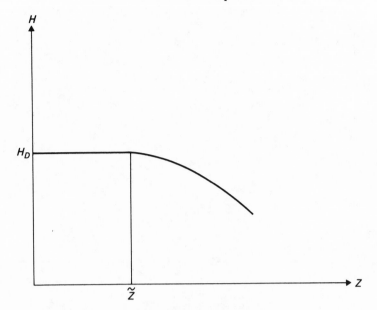

Figure 1
Household demand and purchases as a function of shortage

H_D, and its *actual purchases* by H. The relationship between H and Z is shown in Figure 1.

$$H = H_D, \quad \text{if} \quad Z = 0. \tag{3.9}$$

This is the Walrasian state in which there is no excess demand, not even at the micro-level. If, however, there is some shortage, it compels the households to effectuate forced substitutions. At the micro-level various shortage phenomena are already experienced. These are, however – below a critical shortage intensity $\tilde{Z}$ – compatible with the situation that, at the macro-level, aggregate purchases should still coincide with aggregate demand. (The curve H

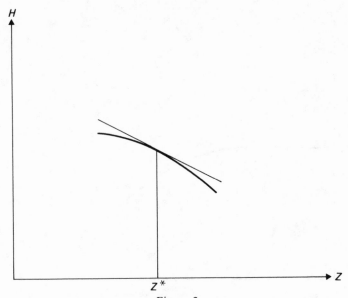

Figure 2
Linearization of the household purchases function

is horizontal.) The household sector spends the income to be used for purchases in a composition different from that originally intended and has to tolerate some of the unpleasant phenomena associated with shortage. Nevertheless, it spends the initially intended amount. However, above the critical value $\tilde{Z}$, shortage begins to discourage households from buying.[10] A higher Z signifies, at the macro-level, that forced substitution, postponement, queuing, and search are increasingly frequent and burdensome at the micro-level. The curve H starts to slope downwards. At the same time, its counterpart also appears in the form of *forced household saving caused by shortage*.

---

[10] An opposite effect is also noticeable, in that shortage may motivate the household to buy more. The curve in Figure 2 represents the joint outcome of the two different effects.

This line of thought leads to the following observation: *household purchases are a non-increasing – and above the critical value $\tilde{Z}$ definitely decreasing – function of shortage.*

In accordance with general assumption 7, we shall linearize the function $H(Z)$ around the value of Z^* corresponding to normal shortage (see Figure 2). The household purchases equation in the model is then as follows:

$$H(t) = H_h^*(t) - \chi_Z(Z(t) - Z^*(t)). \qquad (3.10°)$$

In our equation $H_h^*(t)$ is *the normal value of household purchases.* This depends, as we shall see later, on the income of the household sector. For the time being, $(3.10°)$ only indicates that the household sector buys less than normal if shortage is more intensive than normal, and conversely.

The firms' demand and purchases

I mentioned, in connection with general assumption 4, that the firm's budget constraint is soft and does not bind its purchasing intention. Survival of the firm is guaranteed; if suffering continuous losses, it will sooner or later be rescued from its financial difficulties by a state subsidy, a tax allowance, a credit granted on soft terms, or a centrally approved price increase. The growth of the firm depends only to a limited extent on profitability. As a consequence of all this, the firm's demand for inputs has a tendency to grow without limits.[11] This is all the more so, as the uncertainties of supply caused by shortage motivate firms to *hoard input stocks.*

---

[11] Of course, the budget constraint is not equally soft in every branch or for every firm within the firms' sector. However, since there is a large number of firms where it is definitely soft, it is sufficient for *total* demand of the firms' sector to get out of control.

And yet the firm's demand is not infinite. It is restrained by storage capacity. Besides, superior authorities, the banking system and economic public opinion – which condemn hoarding – put some pressure on the firm to exercise self-restraint. The resulting situation can be described in the following terms: *the firm's demand for current inputs for production is almost insatiable.*

The firms' purchases $Y(t)$ are a function of shortage. The function is shown in Figure 3. As before, since we are dealing with a given year t, we can omit the argument t from the variables.

If normal shortage Z^* is positive, but the economy found itself – by some miracle – in a situation perfectly free of shortage in the year under examination, the firms'

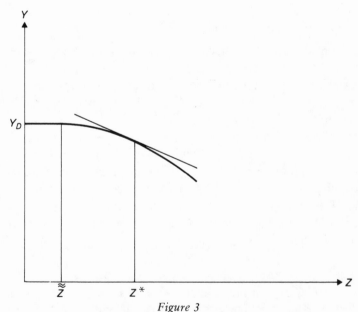

Figure 3
Firms' demand and purchases as a function of shortage

sector could satisfy its demand: $Y = Y_D$. It would fill up all its warehouses and hoard stocks up to the limit tolerated by higher authorities and public opinion.

This is, of course, merely an abstract point in the figure. In a chronic shortage economy there is always shortage. For small positive values of Z, below the critical value[12] $\tilde{\tilde{Z}}$ the function $Y(Z)$ does not yet decrease: even after forced substitutions the firm's purchases expand up to the tolerance limit of hoarding. Above the critical value $\tilde{\tilde{Z}}$, however, such an amount of forced substitution would have to be effected – if the original volume of purchases were insisted on – that it would not be worth the effort, despite a strong hoarding tendency. Too much forced substitution, queuing, and search induces the firm to cut its purchases.

In the final analysis, therefore we may observe that *firm's purchases are a non-increasing – and above the critical value $\tilde{\tilde{Z}}$ definitely decreasing – function of shortage.*

In accordance with general assumption 7, we linearize the function $Y(Z)$ around the value of Z^* corresponding to normal shortage (see Figure 3).

From the theoretical point of view, there is a remarkable analogy with the familiar properties of demand functions as discussed in standard microeconomics. We have the downward-sloping purchases functions H and Y yet not as functions of the purchase price, but of a non-price variable, namely shortage. The loss caused by shortage – concessions made on quality, queuing time, waiting, search, the effort needed to acquire goods – is the 'price' the buyer has to pay. The more intensive the shortage, the higher this 'price', therefore, the more the buyer will refrain from his original purchasing intention.

---

[12] The critical value $\tilde{\tilde{Z}}$ for the firms' sector does not necessarily coincide with the critical value $\tilde{Z}$ for the household sector.

The firms' purchases are described in the model by the following equations:

$$Y(t) = Y^*(t) - \eta_V(V(t) - V^*(t))$$
$$- \eta_Z(Z(t) - Z^*(t)), \tag{3.11°}$$

in which

$$Y^*(t) = \Gamma_Y Y(t-1), \quad \Gamma_Y > 1. \tag{3.12°}$$

The variable $Y^*(t)$ is the *normal value of the firms' purchases*. The growth factor Γ_Y represents the customary growth of the firms' purchases. Actual purchases may deviate from their normal value, as a result of two different effects:

(a) Stock signal. If input stocks have accumulated more than normal, it is worth buying less than the usual amount. Later on we shall see that the normal input stock depends on the volume of production. In the final account, therefore, firms' purchases depend on production, yet this is expressed in a roundabout way in our stock–flow model.

(b) General shortage signal. If shortage intensity is above normal, and consequently the composition of supply is more unfavourable than usual, it is worth buying less than the normal amount.

Production

Let us denote *production* by $X(t)$. This is gross output, produced to cover not only final consumption, but also the current inputs required for production. Its control equation is as follows:

$$X(t) = X^*(t) - \xi_U(U(t) - U^*(t))$$
$$+ \xi_Z(Z(t) - Z^*(t)), \qquad (3.13°)$$

in which $X^*(t)$ is the *normal production*:

$$X^*(t) = p(t) N(t). \qquad (3.14°)$$

In the preceding, the term $p(t)$ denotes *standard productivity*, while $N(t)$ is *employment*. Both will be interpreted later.

Actual production may deviate from its normal value, depending on the effect of two kinds of signal:

(*a*) Stock signal. If the output stock falls below its normal level, production will have to be more than usual.
(*b*) General shortage signal. Intensification of shortage motivates the firms' sector to produce more.

As a matter of fact, both explanatory factors express the 'suction' effect of shortage. Impatient buyers press the producer to supply as much as possible and as soon as possible. In this way, shortage leads to *quantity drive*: overtime work, more night- and weekend-shifts, and other forms of 'rush work'.

The 'suction' effect of shortage in eliciting additional production is felt directly by the managers and employees of the firms, since they are in contact with the buyers urging greater supplies and complaining about forced substitution. All that also affects the superior authorities, who use instructions, as well as a system of rewards and punishments, to stimulate firms to produce larger quantities of output. Equation (3.13°), as well as the other equations describing the behaviour of the sector of firms, represent the joint result of centralized and decentralized influences.

In this relationship, therefore, production is *an increasing function of shortage*. The phrase, 'in this relationship', should be noticed. Here shortage figures as a *signal*, that is as information and stimulus. Later on another relationship will be discussed, in which shortage influences *real* efficiency. That relationship has the opposite sign, in that shortage exerts its influence towards the reduction of output.

At this point we shall digress from describing the equations of the growth model, in order to make one or two theoretical remarks.

Let us introduce the following temporary notation: $\bar{Y}(t)$ is total consumption, therefore, $\bar{Y}(t) = H(t) + Y(t)$. In Figure 4 the purchases function $\bar{Y}(Z)$ and the production

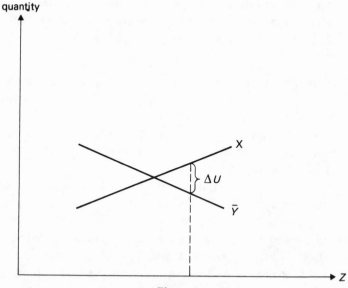

Figure 4
The 'Marshallian cross' in a shortage economy

function $X(Z)$ are shown together (the argument t can be omitted). For the sake of clarity it is assumed that all other conditions are unchanged.

The shape of Figure 4 is familiar: it reminds us of the usual Marshallian cross, with the difference that the horizontal axis shows not the price, but the macroindex of shortage.[13] This is a non-price signal which provides a positive impulse to production and a negative one to purchases. More exactly, in the framework of our macromodel the index Z represents millions of individual shortage phenomena, which collectively influence the decision-makers' behaviour in the directions specified above.

At this point I wish to enter into a controversy with one of my 'predecessors' – E. Malinvaud who gave the Jahnsson lectures in 1977.[14] His study contains – as do all his works – a number of interesting and important ideas, formulated in the lucid and precise manner that is characteristic of him. We share a common interest in non-Walrasian states of economic systems. There are, however, a few matters in which my views differ from his, as well as from the widely represented school to which he refers, associated with the names of Barro, Grossman, Benassy and others.

---

[13] I am pleased to have found a Marshallian cross in a shortage economy market operating without a price signal. This makes it easier for me to remain a member of the 'Econ' tribe whose sacred totem is this cross, as Leijonhufvud demonstrates very wittily in his ethnographical article. (See A. Leijonhufvud, 'Life among the Econ', *Western Economic Journal*, 11 (1973), 327–37.) It is true that different myths are attached to the totem by different members of the tribe, for example, the castes 'Macro' and 'Micro' differ from each other. Therefore, it is possible for a new caste to come forward with a new myth to interpret our common totem.

[14] E. Malinvaud, *The Theory of Unemployment Reconsidered*, Basil Blackwell, Oxford, 1977.

Malinvaud, together with numerous other authors of the school he represents, apply the so-called 'short-side rule' in constructing their models. According to this rule, actual purchases and sales are equal to the smaller of demand and supply. This principle applies, according to these authors, not only at the micro-level but also at the macro-level.

In my opinion, the 'short-side rule' cannot be completely valid even at the micro-level. Forced substitution means precisely that the buyer is forced to purchase a larger quantity of the substitute than that of his original demand. The larger the aggregate to which we apply the rule, the more it will distort any description of the real situation.

Let us remain with the case of a chronic-shortage economy. I shall recall that the purchase curves are downward-sloping. If actual shortage is not far beyond its own normal value, purchases will also not exceed that volume sufficient to absorb completely the economy's output stocks. The output stock is one of the major components of slack in the national economy. In a chronic-shortage economy shortage *and* slack are present simultaneously; and these phenomena are not merely present simultaneously, but a causal relationship exists between them. Shortage encourages the hoarding of input stocks. It is the poor adjustment caused by shortage that leads to the production of goods which the buyers would not accept even for forced substitution. With certain resources shortage creates bottlenecks, which is inevitably accompanied – owing to the rigid complementarity that asserts itself in production in the short run – by the underutilization of other resources.

As a result of these considerations, it is wrong to assert that, as a result of the short-side rule, actual purchases and sales should always coincide with supply in the chronic-shortage economy. *At the macro-level excess demand and excess supply occur simultaneously. Normal shortage Z^* and normal slacks U^*, V^* operate in parallel.* (A more complete model would also take into account other components of normal slack.) *The actual state of the system always fluctuates around these normal levels.*

I wish to illustrate these theoretical and methodological remarks by an example. In their remarkable study on the Eastern-European socialist countries Portes and Winter use the approach of Barro, Grossman, Benassy and Malinvaud; that is, they regard the short-side rule as valid even at the macro-level.[15] I shall quote one of their important findings: There were

> 9 excess demand years for Czechoslovakia (43 per cent of the sample), 13 for the GDR (76 per cent of the sample), 6 for Hungary (32 per cent of the sample) and 5 for Poland (23 per cent of the sample). On this basis excess supply was the dominant regime in three out of the four countries.

In my opinion, the conclusion is absurd. All four countries should be considered chronic-shortage economies all through the period under examination. None of them switched over into a state that could be characterized by 'excess supply'. The only judgement that could be made of each of them is that, *in comparison with their own normal shortage*, actual shortage was sometimes stronger, sometimes weaker. The variable $Z_j(t)$ for each country fluctuated around the national variable $Z_j^*(t)$; (the subscript j refers here to the country).

---

[15] R. Portes and D. Winter, 'Disequilibrium estimates for consumption goods markets in centrally planned economies', *Review of Economic Studies*, 47 (1980), 137–59.

In comparing the Hungarian data used by Portes and Winter with our own shortage macroindex time series given in Appendix C, it appears that the results of the two computations – as regards the directions of upward or downward movement – are not so far apart. The problem is that, when formulating their conclusions, they became entangled in the theoretical and conceptual system applied. That is why they describe the situation as if, in these countries, *qualitative jumps* had occurred several times during the period being studied; that is, shifts from one 'regime' to another, though in fact only *quantitative shifts* occurred, the economies remaining all the time within the same regime.

The two different approaches can also be illustrated graphically. The approach set out in Malinvaud's papers and in the Portes and Winter article is shown in Figure 5. There we see only *one* macrovariable: aggregate excess demand. The jumps between 'regimes' mean that the system is sometimes on the positive, sometimes on the negative part of the same axis; that is to say, to the right and left of the Walrasian equilibrium point.

Figure 6 illustrates the approach of the present model (and that of my earlier works). We see there *two* macro-variables: shortage (Z in the present model), and slack.[16] The normal state of the chronic-shortage economy is a definite point in the positive quadrant, corresponding to a rather strong shortage intensity. In this figure the origin of the co-ordinate system represents the Walrasian point of perfect adjustment. The actual state of the system is always rather distant from this point.

This brings us to an important difference between the two approaches. Figure 5 involves making a very strict assumption. Even if adjustment is not perfect – for either

[16] For the synthetic measurement of slack see footnote 6.

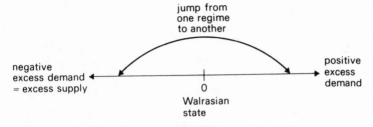

Figure 5
One macrovariable: aggregate excess demand

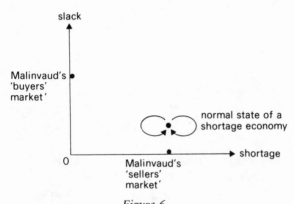

Figure 6
Two macrovariables: shortage and slack

the buyer or the seller is unsatisfied – it is nevertheless at least semi-perfect. The 'shorter side' fulfils its intention perfectly: in case of excess demand the seller sells everything he wishes to, and in case of excess supply the buyer buys everything that he wants. Using the terminology of Barro, Grossman and Malinvaud: an efficient 'rationing' process takes place. The positions of Malinvaud's 'sellers' market' and 'buyers' market' are shown in Figure 6 accordingly.

As opposed to this, the definition of the 'normal state'

in Figure 6 does not involve such a strict assumption, which is rather remote from reality. Instead, it recognizes the fact that real adjustment is not perfect, not even in such a one-sided way. It frequently happens at the micro-level that neither the collectivity of sellers nor that of buyers can perfectly fulfil their intentions. Using the same terminology as above: 'rationing' is not fully efficient. The distance of the normal state from the origin (expressed by an appropriate vector distance measure) indicates the extent of this allocative inefficiency, that is of the friction in the system's adjustment.

Investment

We have now reached the 'core' of the model: the discussion of investment. It may not be exaggerating to say that all macro-theories that neglect a genuine investigation of investment effectively turn their back on the most important question.

Investment is a dynamic process. The implementation of a project goes on for years and, therefore, a micro-level investment decision entails long-term obligations. This is why it is indispensable – even at the cost of some increased complexity in the model's structure – that we should try to represent the *lags* that characterize the investment processes and the associated production processes. This is particularly important in examining the growth problems of the Eastern-European socialist countries since, as is well known, the protracted implementation of investment projects is quite frequent.[17]

[17] Table B.2 of Appendix B draws a comparison between Hungarian and Japanese data, demonstrating that construction periods in Hungary are a multiple of those in Japan. This is a consequence of chronic shortage: frequent delays in supplies, shortages of building material, labour, etc.

Our model does not contain aggregate capital. On the one hand, we distinguish between fixed and current assets, and within the latter between input and output stocks – as was made clear earlier. As regards fixed capital, it is represented by the well-known 'vintage' model. We do not aggregate fixed capital of different vintages, but treat each vintage separately.[18]

We assume that investments are only made in the sector of state- or co-operative-owned firms, and that they are exclusively for productive purposes. All investments from other sources or for other purposes are disregarded.

The concepts and relationships connected with investment vintages are illustrated in Figure 7. The totality of investment projects begun in year t is called the tth *investment vintage*. The various projects are not all completed together; the implementation period of the project taking the longest time defines the *gestation period* for the whole vintage. It is assumed that this is identical for every vintage Let us denote it by G; in Figure 7 this is 6 years. In our model the gestation period G is an exogenous parameter.

We assume that production with the newly created fixed assets begins at the end of the gestation period. That is, the tth investment vintage contributes to production from the $(t + G)$th year, as shown in Figure 7.

---

[18] In modelling investment, I was influenced by several sources: Austrian capital theory in the form revived by J. R. Hicks, works by R. F. Harrod and Leif Johansen, the vintage models of R. M. Solow, T. W. Swan, N. Kaldor and J. A. Mirlees, the Oslo Model of Ragnar Frisch, and Joan Robinson's criticism of the neoclassical aggregate capital concept – to mention just the most important ones. In Hungary, M. Augusztinovics and T. Faur have dealt with the modelling of the investment lag-structure. In formulating the variables and equations describing the real investment process, I sought to combine some of the ideas of the above authors.

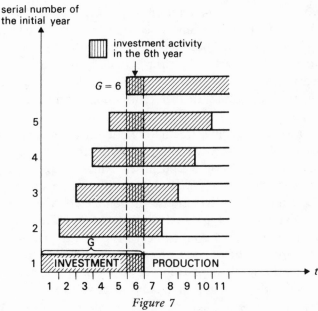

Figure 7
The vintage approach and the gestation period

The *volume* of the tth vintage is denoted by $M(t)$. The variable $M(t)$ 'symbolizes' the machines and buildings put into operation as a result of projects started in year t. This volume could be measured in several ways. For purposes of theoretical analysis the following interpretation will be suitable: $M(t)$ is the *ex-ante* estimate of the expenditure needed to complete the given investment vintage, based on engineers' calculations. We shall see later on that the actual investment input may differ from this.

Let us now consider a single vintage. The expenditure on each project has its own particular dynamics; one lasts longer, the other one a shorter time; in one much expenditure is incurred at the beginning, in another in the middle of the gestation period, and so on. Summing up all ex-

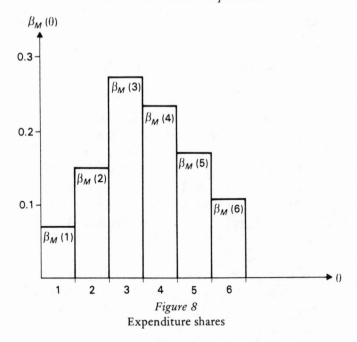

Figure 8
Expenditure shares

penditures in each year of the period of length G, we obtain the pattern of expenditure for the totality of all projects of that vintage. This is illustrated in Figure 8, which is based on a numerical estimate reflecting Hungarian experience. Let us denote by $\beta_M(\theta)$ the *expenditure share* of the vintage in year θ. Expenditure begins in year 1. Clearly,

$$\sum_{\theta=1}^{G} \beta_M(\theta) = 1.$$

Again we introduce a strong assumption: the series $\beta_M(1)$, ..., $\beta_M(G)$ are considered exogenous parameters identical for every vintage, unchanged over time. Accordingly, the investment outlays in year t are:

$$\tilde{B}(t) = \sum_{0}^{G-1} \beta_M(\theta + 1) M(t - \theta).$$

Vintage t is described, in addition to the above-mentioned volume variable $M(t)$, by two further variables. One is $J(t)$, the *number of jobs* created by the investment vintage; the other is $q(t)$, the *vintage productivity*. The latter is the productivity of labour in the jobs created by vintage t. Just as for $M(t)$, so also $J(t)$ and $q(t)$ are *pre-estimates* based upon engineers' calculations. Actual employment and productivity may, as we shall see later, deviate from them.

We assume that there is no disembodied technical progress. It is unnecessary to enquire at this point whether this is true. It does not seem to be too difficult to develop the model further in the direction of incorporating some form of technical progress not embodied in fixed capital. Yet now, that is when taking the initial steps in constructing the model, it seems unnecessary to complicate the structure of the model any more. Technical development is therefore formalized in the simplest possible terms.

$$J(t) = \chi\Phi^t M(t), \quad 0 < \Phi < 1, \qquad (3.15^\circ)$$

in which χ is the *initial job-creation coefficient*, and Φ is the job-creation growth factor. The formula does express the well-known tendency whereby, as a result of technical progress, the number of jobs created by a unit of investment input declines from vintage to vintage.

$$q(t) = \lambda\Psi^t, \quad \Psi > 1, \qquad (3.16^\circ)$$

in which λ is the *initial vintage labour productivity coefficient*, and Ψ is the vintage labour productivity growth factor. This formula also expresses a familiar tendency: as a result of technical progress, the productivity of labour working with the newest machines grows from vintage to vintage.

Technical progress has been described in both equations using the simplest exponential forms, implying a *constant rate* of progress. Of course, the introduction of the expressions $(3.15°)$ and $(3.16°)$ does not imply that in the model the actual job-investment ratio, or the actual labour productivity, change at a constant rate from year to year. The actual ratios will depend on many things, including the volume of the different vintages. The two formulae only describe the exponential change in the employment and productivity *possibilities* latent in the techniques introduced by successive vintages.

In reality, the *technical parameters* χ, Φ, λ and Ψ are not independent of each other. Their interrelations are treated in detail in theories of production and growth. However, we do not deal with these interrelationships here. We wish, with the aid of our model, to focus attention primarily on the development of the *volume* of investment. Therefore, we have constructed the model so that *the control of the investment volume in it should take place endogenously*. On the other hand, we refrain from modelling the *choice of technique* endogenously. (In the present mathematical formalism this could only be investigated with difficulty, if at all.) Therefore, *the parameters reflecting technical progress are considered exogenous*. The most we can do – and we shall indeed do it – is to make comparative calculations, assuming different sets of parameters χ, Φ, λ and Ψ, thereby simulating alternative paths of technical progress.

In the preceding part of the section we outlined how to

model the *real* process of investment. Now we shall go on to describe its *control*.[19] First, let us define the variable $K(t)$, representing *investment commitment*.

$$K(t) = \sum_{\theta=1}^{G-1} \sum_{\tau=\theta+1}^{G} \beta_M(\tau)\, M(t-\theta). \qquad (3.17^\circ)$$

Instead of giving a verbal explanation, we present Figure 9, which shows clearly what we call investment commitment for year t. We can now write down the control equation governing the investment process:

$$M(t) = M^*(t) + \mu_H(H(t-1) - H^*_{\text{plan}}(t-1))$$
$$- \mu_K(K(t) - K^*(t)) \qquad (3.18^\circ)$$
$$- \mu_Z(Z(t) - Z^*(t)).$$

First we shall comment on the left-hand side: the specification of the *variable to be controlled*. The model of the real investment process indicates how much investment expenditure is due in year t. (This is emphasized in Figure 7

[19] On the control of the investment process in a socialist economy T. Bauer has written an important wide-ranging book, at present under publication. The manuscript was mimeographed by the Institute of Economics of the Hungarian Academy of Sciences in 1977 under the title: *A beruházási volumen a közvetlen tervgazdálkodásban* [Investment Volume in the Directly Planned Economy]. Some of the propositions in the book are in a previously published article: 'Investment cycles in planned economies', *Acta Oeconomica*, 21 (1978), 243–60.

A few other significant works have been published on the subject in Hungary. Thus, for example, A. K. Soós, 'Causes of investment fluctuations', *Eastern-European Economics*, 14(2) (1975–76), 25–36, and M. Lackó, 'Cumulating and easing of tensions', *Acta Oeconomica*, 24 (1980), No. 3–4.

I have used some of Bauer's, Soós' and Lackó's thoughts in constructing my model of investments.

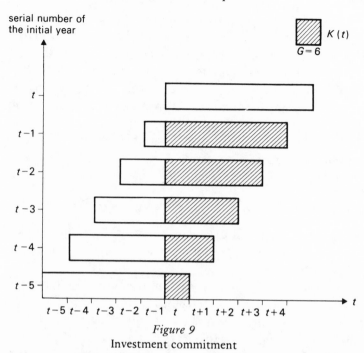

Figure 9
Investment commitment

for the 6th year: it is the double-striped column above the 6th year.) And yet we consider that this is *not* the control variable of greatest importance. Once a project is initiated, it is usually not finally stopped, particularly in a socialist economy. The decisive question, therefore, concerns how many projects, and of what volume, *are started*. This is expressed in the model by $M(t)$, in an aggregate form. It is true that the implementation of projects under way, or the fulfilment of commitments, can be accelerated or slowed down in the course of their progress. If, however, the structure of the model is to be simplified, we shall have to disregard *this* control possibility. On the other hand, we do not want to disregard the lag effects; that is, that the total investment expenditure incurred in year t was substantially decided in years $(t - 1)$, $(t - 2)$, ..., $(t - G + 1)$, when the volume of the still unfinished vintages was originally determined. The investment decision-maker is to a large extent constrained by his earlier decisions. This is the extremely important phenomenon that is omitted from those models which only contain the customary macrovariable $I(t)$, that is, the amount that is spent from production of year t on investment inputs in that year.

Now let us proceed to the right-hand side of the formula, and to its first term, $M^*(t)$, which is the *normal volume of the investment vintage*.

$$M^*(t) = \Gamma_M M^*(t-1) = \Gamma_M^t M_0, \quad \Gamma_M > 1, \quad (3.19°)$$

in which M_0 is the initial value of year 0 of the normal value of the investment vintage, and Γ_M is the corresponding growth factor.

Formula ($3.19°$) reflects – within the formal structure of our model – an important regularity of the socialist economy. *On average, over a long period, the economic management organs consider growth at a constant rate as normal.* Since in our model the control variable of the investment process is $M(t)$, this 'normality postulate' manifests itself in the exponential character of the normal path of the vintage volumes, $M^*(t)$.

Three kinds of feedback are operating.[20] We do not

[20] The present description of the feedback control of investments is similar to the model of O. Kyn, W. Schrettl and J. Slama. (See the study 'Growth cycles in centrally planned economies: an empirical test', in O. Kyn and W. Schrettl (eds), *On the Stability of Contemporary Economic Systems*, Vandenhoeck-Ruprecht, Göttingen, 1979.) In their model the investment decision also responds to deviations from the normal path. They also support their propositions econometrically, using Czechoslovakian data.

Since the study in question does not make any reference to previous works of the present author and his colleagues, it seems that they arrived at their approach, in many respects similar to ours, independently of us.

claim that in reality the lag structure of the various feed-backs is as simple as that shown in formula (3.18°), since in practice distributed lags would assert themselves. Yet the simple structure given above seems adequate for the present theoretical analysis, for it makes clear our main point about the causal direction of 'signal–reaction' inter-relations.

For an explanation of the *first feedback*, we must define the variable $H^*_{\text{plan}}(t)$ that is *the normal value of consumption*.

$$H^*_{\text{plan}}(t) = \Gamma_H H(t - 1), \quad \Gamma_H > 1, \qquad (3.20°)$$

in which Γ_H is the growth factor of normal consumption. Attention is drawn to the fact that in our model household purchases (that is consumption, since we consider this to equal purchases) assume two different normal values. The first normal value, $H^*_h(t)$ is deduced from the real income and savings of households. (This has already been mention-ed, and we shall revert to it in more detail later.) The second normal value can be seen in the preceding formula. It is $H^*_{\text{plan}}(t)$, incorporating the norms of economic policy and planning. The former is determined 'below', in the household sphere, while the latter 'above', in the sphere of economic management, that is among central planners. Let us now discuss the latter.

In formulating economic policy, it must be taken into account that the population expects its consumption to rise, now and in the future, at the customary rate. Accord-ingly, the first feedback in formula (3.18°) reflects the behaviour of the central economic policy-makers and planners. *If the growth of consumption remains below its usual rate, the scale of investment will be reduced so as to leave more of the national income for consumption. If, on the other hand, the population 'lives too well', or the*

*growth of consumption has accelerated unusually, larger
volumes of investments can be started, since it is considered justified to divert some of the resources devoted to
household consumption.*

It can be verified empirically that this kind of feedback
exists, though not necessarily in the very simple form that
appears in the model. In his work on investment in socialist
countries, mentioned already, T. Bauer calls this kind of
reaction 'a cycle symmetrical with consumption'. Figure
10 has been taken from one of his works,[21] for illustration.

The *second feedback* influences upper-, medium-, and
lower-level decision-makers alike. It involves *the normal
value of investment commitment*:

$$K^*(t) = \Gamma_K K(t - 1), \quad \Gamma_K > 1, \qquad (3.21°)$$

in which Γ_K is the growth factor of the normal investment
commitment. *If economic managers feel they have over-
committed themselves in the past, they will now hold back
new investment starts.*

The *third feedback* is based on the shortage signal. If
$Z(t) > Z^*(t)$, this will certainly be noticeable in the field
of investments: the supply of machines to be installed
suffers longer and more frequent delays, material or labour
shortage creates increasing difficulty for building opera-
tions or the installation of machines. In addition, when an
investment project is completed more than the usual
obstacles are encountered in putting the new capacity into

---

[21] The same idea is confirmed by the investigations of several authors
covering other socialist countries. See, for example, B. Mieczkowski
'The relationship between changes in consumption and politics in
Poland', *Soviet Studies*, 30 (1978), 262–9, and V. Bunce 'The
political consumption cycle: a comparative analysis', *Soviet Studies*,
32 (1980), 280-90.

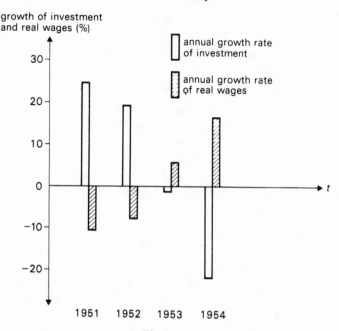

Figure 10
Investment and real wages (Hungarian data)
Source: T. Bauer, 'Beruházási ciklusok a tervgazdaságban' [Investment cycles in the planned economy], *Gazdaság*, 12 (4) (1978), 57–75

operation. Because of rush work caused by shortage, the teething troubles of new plant may be prolonged, and so on.[22] More intense shortage reflects the fact that the system meets its own resource constraints more and more

[22] In regard to the second and third feedback, certain phenomena are involved which were discussed by Branko Horvat in his valuable studies ('The optimum rate of investment', *Economic Journal*, 68 (1958), 747–67; and 'The rule of accumulation in a planned economy', *Kyklos*, 21 (1968), 239–68). Horvat discussed the constraints on the *investment-absorption capacity* of the system. The system is unable to 'digest' efficiently an over-ambitious investment programme, or the new capacities it creates.

frequently and suffers increasing losses. *Above-normal shortage intensity therefore induces the decision-makers to restrain new investment starts.* Conversely, if the difficulties caused by shortage, including the backlog of orders for the building and machine industry, have diminished and complaints about under-utilization are beginning to be voiced, this will provide a stimulus to expand investment activity.[23]

Summing up: *three different non-price signals have been described. As a result of their influence, decision-makers cause $M(t)$ to deviate from its normal value $M^*(t)$ so as to drive the system back to the normal paths of consumption, investment and shortage.*

Our model reveals an important phenomenon characteristic of the Eastern-European socialist economies which we call *expansion drive*, and the concomitant *investment hunger*. It will be easier to understand, if we make a comparison with the capitalist economy.

In the capitalist system, investment intentions are constrained by the firm's concern about *risk*. If the additional capacity created by some investment exceeded by too much the growth in demand, the investment would fail and the firm would go bankrupt. The decision-maker is largely influenced by expectations of future selling possibilities and future profitability.[24] Still, these are *'self-fulfilling' expectations*. For fear of the risks, investment is

---

[23] The previously mentioned works of Bauer, Soós and Lackó support the hypotheses concerned with the second and third feedback. Lackó discerns two 'tensions': internal tension caused by investment commitment, and external tension caused by a foreign trade balance worse than normal. It would be worth including the latter in the control equation ($3.17°$), if we come to build foreign trade into the growth model.

[24] See for example R. Eisner, *Factors in Business Investment*, Ballinger, Cambridge, Mass., 1978.

cautious, as is the expansion of production that follows in its wake, and this requires a moderate growth rate of demand. This also makes future profitability more uncertain, however, precisely because of the uncertainties of sales. The final result is that investment intentions, that is the demand for investment resources, are voluntarily restrained by decision-makers.

In the Eastern-European socialist economies, the attitude towards investment is vastly different. The decision-maker does not experience any concern about the financial risks of his investment. As for sales, the chronic-shortage economy ensures that every (or almost every) product is saleable sooner or later. We can therefore see here too a form of 'self-fulfilling' expectation, but based on a more optimistic and faster growth rate: since the expansion of investment is rapid, production and demand grow correspondingly quickly. And, as far as finances are concerned, if for some reason (such as excessive investment or operating costs or lower than expected selling prices) financial losses were suffered as a consequence of the investment project, the state would bail the firm out. It is the lack of genuine risk that accounts for the fact that for firms, non-profit institutions, lower- and medium-level managers, and sectoral leaders there is no *self-imposed* limit to the demand for investment resources. That is why we say that the *demand for investment goods is almost insatiable*.

Keynes justly spoke of the entrepreneur's animal spirits which, if dimmed, would lead to the fading of investment enterprise. From this point of view, a statistical comparison of investment data for a few European socialist and capitalist countries will be useful. We have taken such capitalist countries as Austria, Denmark, Finland, Greece, Ireland, Italy and Spain, whose development level is comparable to that of the socialist countries selected for the sample (Bulgaria, Poland, Hungary and the GDR). The

5 years before and after the 'oil-shock' will be compared (see Table B.3 of Appendix B). The difference is quite dramatic: the growth rate of investment in the period from 1973 to 1977 did not show any significant change in the socialist countries, while it slowed down considerably in most of the capitalist countries listed above. The investment spirit of the capitalist entrepreneur was held in check by the poor economic prospects, which certainly intensified the slow-down or decline in production and hence moderated the growth rate of demand, which again weakened the investment spirit, and so on. On the other side, the 'vital instinct' for investment did not decline at all on the part of the 'entrepreneurs' in socialist countries: the initiators of investments, that is those applying for state investment subsidies and credits. The fact that, for example, the rise in energy prices or growing difficulties in exporting to capitalist countries may adversely affect the future efficiency of investments did not diminish the investment spirit in the least.

To avoid misunderstanding, it should be stressed that we are talking about investment *intention*, the *initiation* of projects, and the *demand* for investment resources. It is another question – which, however, is not the point here – that exporting difficulties resulting from the 'oil-shock', the worsening terms of trade, and the stagnation–recession in capitalist countries affect, of course, the Eastern-European countries listed above. They exert an unfavourable effect on the efficiency of production and foreign trade. Sooner or later, therefore, some slow-down in investment and correspondingly, in the growth rate of production, will become inevitable. This is already reflected in data on the recent past, the present and in the plans concerning the near future. Yet this effect entered these economies through the *real* sphere and not directly and without delay influencing the *control* sphere. On seeing the less favourable prospects, decision-makers did not immediately change their behaviour, and it was only after several years' delay that investment ambitions subsided and new norms were formed.[25] In fact, it was not the investment *spirit* that subsided, but everybody was forced to acknowledge that the *physical potential* for investment activities had become more limited.

After glimpsing some of the reality of economic history, we can return to the model's investment control equation $(3.18°)$. Our model seeks to reflect in two different ways what I explained above about the expansionary investment behaviour prevailing in a socialist economy. First, in the term $M^*(t)$ which prescribes – as I pointed out – the customary and persistent expansion thought normal by everybody. Second, the formula also reflects system-specific behaviour in its deliberate *omission* of certain explanatory variables. *The volume of investment does not depend on the financial state of the firms' sector, its present and future profits, accumulated or additional savings, the condition of the state budget, or any expected constraints on sales. It would be a mistake to omit these factors from a growth model of a capitalist economy – just as it would be a mistake to include them in the present model.*

---

[25] If the system is unable to grow any further at its customary rate – because of various external or internal factors – but can only grow at a different rate, for example, more slowly, this will be expressed in our conceptual system in the following way: the *norms of the system would have shifted*. In the present model this can be formalized so as to replace the growth factors Γ_M, Γ_H, Γ_K, etc. and other parameters by a set of parameters taking different numerical values.

Employment

Let us denote the *economic life* (or durability) of fixed capital by T. It is assumed (a strong simplification) that the eonomic life of the fixed capital installed by every investment vintage is identical.

In the model T is an exogenous parameter. In reality the date of scrapping machines, or demolishing buildings would be determined by numerous economic decisions. Within the framework of the current formulation, however, it is impossible to treat economic life as an endogenous control variable.

The fixed capital created by the investment vintage started in year t contributes to production in year $(t + G)$ and ends its contribution in year $(t + G + T - 1)$. After that it is dismantled or demolished.

Labour demand, denoted by $L_D(t)$, is given by the following equation:

$$L_D(t) = \sum_{\theta = G}^{T + G - 1} J(t - \theta). \qquad (3.22^\circ)$$

Labour demand is determined by the job-creating effect of the various investment vintages, summing over the vintages in operation in year t.

For the time being – throughout Chapter 3 – we are discussing the so-called *extensive growth period* of the socialist economy. At that time labour reserves were still large, above all because of the low employment of the village population and of female labour. Labour supply could be considered practically unlimited.[26] Accordingly,

---

[26] This is only approximately true. In certain jobs, or in certain geographical regions, labour shortage was already perceived in that period.

actual employment, $N(t)$ coincides with labour demand:

$$N(t) = L_D(t). \qquad (3.23°)$$

A subsequent chapter discusses the exhaustion of labour reserves: *the intensive growth period*. We explain there the necessary replacement for equation $(3.23°)$, and other modifications that have to be made to the equation system in order to represent the intensive period.

It is a characteristic of the extensive period that while the market for products is a 'sellers' market' with chronic shortage, the market for labour is a 'buyers' market' with substantial labour reserves.

Real wages and household savings

As already mentioned in commenting on general assumption 4, we assumed, in constructing the model, that the household does not react separately to nominal incomes and the consumer price level. Its decisions about spending and saving depend exclusively on their joint effect; that is, on real wages. (We disregard other types of income.)

The real wage fund is denoted by $W(t)$. It is determined by the following equation:

$$W(t) = W^*(t) - \omega_H(H(t-1) - H^*_{\text{plan}}(t-1)). \quad (3.24°)$$

The first explanatory variable is $W^*(t)$, the *normal value of the real wage fund*:

$$W^*(t) = \omega_N \Omega^t N(t), \qquad (3.25°)$$

in which ω_N is the *initial real wage rate* (the yearly total real wage per employee), and Ω is the growth factor of the normal real wage fund. The *per capita* normal wage fund multiplied by employment, $N(t)$, determines the normal real wage fund.

In the control of the real wage fund central policy on living standards and the pressure on real wages exerted by employees both have some effect. The actual real wage fund may deviate from its normal value as a consequence of a feedback mechanism. The variable $H^*_{plan}(t)$ has already appeared in the control equation for the investment volume (3.18°). It represents the exponential normal path of household consumption. The logic of the feedback is then as follows: if in the previous year actual household consumption lagged behind its normal value, the present year's real wages would rise at a higher rate.

And now we are in a position to provide an explanation for $H^*_h(t)$ also, which we did not do when interpreting equation (3.10°) representing household consumption.

$$H^*_h(t) = \chi_W W(t), \qquad (3.26)$$

in which χ_W is the *normal spending ratio of the household*, assuming that actual shortage is just at its normal level: $Z(t) = Z^*(t)$. Its complement, $(1 - \chi_W)$, is the *normal household savings ratio*. This already includes a certain amount of forced saving caused by shortage, since some forced saving occurs even at the normal level of shortage. For the sake of simplification, it is assumed that χ_W does not change over time and that it is independent of $W(t)$. In the model it is an exogenous parameter.

Now we rewrite the household purchases equation (3.10°):

$$
\begin{aligned}
H(t) &= H^*_h(t) - \chi_Z(Z(t) - Z^*(t)) \\
&= \chi_W W(t) - \chi_Z(Z(t) - Z^*(t)).
\end{aligned}
\qquad (3.27)
$$

It turns out that household savings, that is the difference $(W(t) - H(t))$ (i.e. the difference between equations (3.24°) and (3.27)) are explained in a rather complex way. Household savings *depend on the normal wage rate and its growth rate (these are exogenous parameters); in addition, savings depend on the adjustment of real wages determined by the difference between actual and of normal consumption paths, on employment, and finally, on shortage intensity.*

Accumulated savings influence household demand and purchases. This relationship is disregarded in the model.

Input–output relations

First we set out the equation for *current inputs*:

$$A(t) = \alpha_X X(t) + \alpha_Z(Z(t) - Z^*(t)), \qquad (3.28°)$$

in which α_X is the *current input coefficient*, when shortage is normal. If shortage is more severe than that, more current inputs will be necessary: losses caused by forced substitution will be larger, there will be more waste, etc. Here $Z(t)$ is not a signal, but it has a *real* effect on the input–output ratios in production.

And now let us come to the equation for *investment inputs*:

$$B(t) = \sum_{\theta=0}^{G-1} \beta_M(\theta + 1) M(t - \theta) + \beta_Z(Z(t) - Z^*(t)). \quad (3.29°)$$

The first term on the right-hand side represents the expected investment $\tilde{B}(t)$ defined earlier, namely the investment inputs required in year t, according to estimates made at the start of the investment vintage, based on engineers' calculations. These calculations are based upon the assumption of a normal intensity of shortage. The second term introduces a correction to cover situations where actual shortage is more or less severe than normal.

In the *control* equation (3.18°) shortage appears as a signal which influences decision-maker's behaviour in determining the investment vintage volume $M(t)$. As opposed to this, in the *real* equation (3.29°) the *real* effects of shortage are represented; these raise, or lower the investment inputs, $B(t)$ above or below their normal level. For example, if shortage is more intensive than usual, irregular material supply, delays in the delivery of machines, etc., add to the costs of investment.[27]

In its economic content, it is the variable $B(t)$ that comes closest to what is usually denoted by I in standard macromodels and called 'investment'. (Though the latter also includes our stock increments; that is the amount $(\Delta U(t) + \Delta V(t))$.) At this point I should repeat what I stressed already in commenting on equation (3.18°): the present model represents reality more correctly, in that it *does not* consider the variable $B(t)$ as a control variable. Thus $B(t)$ is for the most part predetermined by $M(t-1)$, $\ldots, M(t-G+1)$, and is also strongly influenced by $Z(t)$, which again is not a control variable but is in turn determined by several other variables. It is only the control variable $M(t)$ which can be determined simultaneously with $B(t)$ and which still affects $B(t)$ directly. This effect, however, is rather weak, since only a certain fraction of

[27] Shortage also influences investment efficiency in numerous other ways. We shall mention just one of them: intensification of shortage leads to the protraction of investments. In reality, therefore, the gestation period G is not constant, but is a function of shortage: $G(Z)$. Within the framework of the chosen formulation, however, we cannot express this interrelation.

the investment outlays induced by the vintage volume $M(t)$ actually occur in the initial year t.[28]

My remarks on equations (3.18°) and (3.29°) should throw some light on the motives that prompted me – formal–technical difficulties notwithstanding – to incorporate into the model the rather complicated lag structure associated with investment. Had I not done this, but had instead been content merely to use the standard macro-equation, $Y = C + I$ (national income is equal to consumption plus investment), with investment treated as exogenous, the model would certainly be much simpler. But then it could hardly be used satisfactorily as a description of the internal motion and regulation of economy, or for analysing interrelations between short- and long-term changes. Nor would it be suitable for demonstrating the specific inertia of the investment process, resulting from its characteristic reaction lags.[29]

The third input–output equation is concerned with the output/labour ratio.

[28] In fact, the completion of investments started earlier and already under way can be accelerated or decelerated to a certain extent. Thus, finally, the fraction of the total investment volume controllable during year t by decisions made in the same year t is composed of two items: (1) deviations caused by acceleration towards or deceleration away from investment outlays due in year t as a consequence of earlier decisions; and (2) that part of the investment vintage started in year t due in the first year. Even the sum of these two items will only be a fragment of total investment activity going on in year t.

[29] Lags play an important role in explaining the *investment cycle* occurring in socialist countries. Our model might be used for the theoretical study of such cycles. The present book, however, does not discuss this topic.

$$p(t) = \sum_{\theta = G}^{T+G-1} J(t - \theta) \, q(t - \theta) \Bigg/ \sum_{\theta = G}^{T+G-1} J(t - \theta)$$

$$-(\Psi^t / \Gamma_Z^t) \, \pi_Z (Z(t) - Z^*(t)). \tag{3.30°}$$

The first term on the right-hand side is a weighted average of the vintage productivities; weighted according to the shares of the different vintages in the fixed capital of year t. The higher the share of comparatively recent vintages, the higher the value of the overall ratio. Let us call this production/labour ratio *technical productivity*. It is constructed from preliminary estimates based on engineers' calculations, made in the expectation that shortage would be of normal intensity.

The second term corrects this measure of technical productivity according to whether the actual shortage is stronger or weaker than normal.[30] If it is stronger, productivity declines because of the frequent disturbances in materials and spare-parts supply, technological improvisations entailed by forced substitutions, etc. Let us denote by $p(t)$ the technical productivity adjusted to allow for the real effects of shortage and call it *standard productivity*.

We recall the fact that standard productivity, multiplied by actual employment, appeared earlier in equation $(3.14°)$ determining normal production: $X^*(t) = p(t) \, N(t)$.

The structure of the model allows *actual* productivity to deviate from *standard* productivity; thus $X(t)/N(t)$ can be either larger or smaller than $p(t)$. Such deviations can arise if $X(t)$ differs from $X^*(t)$ and/or $N(t)$ differs from $\Sigma J(t - \theta)$.

---

[30] The factor Ψ^t/Γ_Z^t must be included only as a 'technical trick'. At this point we must – to conform to the productivity term expressed as a ratio – effect in this way the 'scaling up' which we accounted for when explaining equations (3.5)–(3.7) on p. 23.

Stocks

We have now defined all the variables needed to formulate the allocation balance equations.

Balance equation for *output stocks*:

$$U(t) = U(t-1) + X(t-1) - Y(t-1) - H(t-1). \qquad (3.31°)$$

The equation determining *normal output stocks*:

$$U^*(t) = \rho(H(t-1) + Y(t-1)), \qquad (3.32°)$$

in which ρ is the *normal output stock coefficient*.

Balance equation for *input stocks*:

$$V(t) = V(t-1) + Y(t-1) - A(t-1) - B(t-1) \qquad (3.33°)$$

The equation determining *normal input stocks*:

$$V^*(t) = \sigma(A(t-1) + B(t-1)), \qquad (3.34°)$$

in which σ is the *normal input stock coefficient*.

It is useful to explain here the importance of distinguishing between output and input stocks. This is not a distinction related to the physical properties of the product, but it is concerned with *who disposes* of the stock: whoever produced it as an output, or someone else wanting to use it as an input.

(1) As already stressed on p. 4 when I was dealing with the main properties of the model, I want the *interactions between stock and flow variables to be displayed consistently in the model*. Therefore, in contrast to many other models, we strictly separate production and sales on the output side, and purchases and use (productive con-

sumption) on the input side. This separation in terms of flow variables is reflected in the stock variables, by their separation into two different stocks: the output stock is inserted between production and sales, and input stocks come between purchases and productive consumption.

Although in practice this separation is not always easy to make, experience suggests that it is not impossible.

(2) Output stocks and input stocks play different roles in the *signal system* of the economy. The control of production responds to output stocks, while the control of purchases responds to input stocks.

(3) In different socioeconomic systems we can observe fundamentally different regularities in the ratios of U and V, and correspondingly, of ρ and σ.

In the socialist economy I am describing conditions of 'suction' prevail: 'pulling out' the output stock from the warehouses of the producer–seller. It is true that the warehouse is not totally emptied since, not least because of friction and flagging interest on the part of sellers, there are products which buyers will not accept even in forced substitution. In any case, under conditions of 'suction' output stocks are usually no more than the minimum quantity implied by the time necessary to complete transactions, plus a barely saleable frozen stock. As opposed to this, input stocks are large as a consequence of the hoarding tendency stimulated by shortage.

In a capitalist economy (on average over the cycle) the proportions tend to be different. The system is demand-constrained, and this may lead to the expansion of output stocks. At the same time, material purchases and the supply of other inputs are quite smooth; therefore, it is not usually necessary to hoard input stocks.[31]

[31] The capitalist firm may try to hoard input stocks if it expects a rise in input prices.

The above propositions are supported by empirical data, but they can also be confirmed by deduction from the behavioural regularities that assert themselves in the two different mechanisms. Table B.4 of Appendix B shows that the share of output stocks in total stocks is two or three times larger in capitalist countries than in socialist countries.

We must draw attention to the fact that *an explicit 'rationing scheme' is not built into our model*. Firms' demand for current inputs, or for investment inputs and the demand of households for consumer articles compete with each other for X, the total production of the economy – without the model containing a rule to determine the fulfilment proportions of the three different purchasing intentions.

The share of consumption is greatly influenced by the two main distributional parameters in the model: ω_N, the initial real wage rate, and Ω the normal growth factor of the real wage fund. The share of accumulation is affected by a series of parameters: the normal growth factors of the investment volume and of the investment commitment, stock norms, etc.

Aside from the effect of these parameters *the various feedback mechanisms functioning in the model ensure that the allocation cannot deviate persistently from its normal proportions*.

If too much output is allocated to one area in some year, feedbacks ensure that in the following year less should be allocated there, and more to other areas. If household purchases lagged behind last year, this checks investment – by means of the feedback – so that more output is available for households. If input stocks have accumulated too much firms' purchases will slow down, and so on.

This kind of autonomous movement, including internal

control mechanisms, takes place not only in the model, but in the practice of the socialist economy as well. (Obviously, in a much more complicated way, since our macromodel can only illustrate the extremely complicated reality in a very simplified way.) However, in connection with 'autonomous movement' and 'internal control', we must beware of a 'decentralized' and one-sided interpretation of these concepts. May I recall the conception introduced on p. 8: in constructing the model we consider the economic policy-maker, the planner, and the central manager as endogenous parts of the system. *Thus the behavioural regularities and feedback mechanisms described in the model represent the combined reactions of all the levels participating in multi-level control.*

Now we have reached the end of the description and interpretation of the model. A summary of the model is given in Appendix A.

4

Some General Properties of the Model

Simple properties

Analysis of the model is initiated by setting forth a few simple properties. They do not lead to any economic conclusions, yet it is important to be aware of them, for they serve as a starting-point for later investigation.

(1) In mathematical form, the model is a set of non-homogeneous difference equations. Equations (A.8), (A.10) and (A.18) are bilinear, otherwise they are all linear.[2]

(2) The set of equations can be solved *recursively*.[3] This is a remarkable property from more than one standpoint. It simplifies computer simulation. In case of econo-

---

[1] András Simonovits has carried out some mathematical analysis of the model which is not included in this book; however, his conclusions are used. Several of the propositions of Chapters 4 and 5 are the results of our joint work.

[2] At this point, as well as in the remainder of the book, with the exception of pp. 110–14, equations are referred to according to their numbers in Appendix A.

[3] Recursive computations are possible – in the present case – if there exists an ordering 1, 2, . . . , $(i-1)$, i, $(i+1)$, . . . , of the equations,

metric application, parameter estimation may be more straightforward than usual. It might be helpful in economic analysis, throwing light on the direction of causal linkages.

(3) We must provide initial values for $(T + G + 7)$ variables.[4] When this is done, *all variables of the system are uniquely determined for all time $t \geqq 1$*. This means that our model satisfies a primary condition for tractability: it is a well-defined, dynamic model capable of describing uniquely the dynamics of the system as it evolves over time.

(4) The growth model described in Chapter 3 and in Appendix A consists of 26 equations with 26 unknowns. Let us call it the *detailed* model. The model can be 'compressed', in the following way:

Six variables are selected, and referred to hereafter as the *fundamental variables*: these are the output stock U, the input stock V, the deviation of actual shortage from its normal value, $\hat{Z} = Z - Z^*$, the volume of the investment vintage M, the firms' purchases Y and household purchases

---

which has the following property:

In equation i for year t there is a single unknown; all the other variables in the equation have been previously determined, either with the aid of an equation for year t with a number less than i in the ordering, or with the aid of an equation with a higher number, but for a year prior to year t.

The recursive order of the equations in the 26-equation model differs from the order introduced in Chapter 3 as well as from that of Appendix A.

[4] The following initial values must be specified: $M(t)$, for $t = 0, -1, -2, \ldots, (-G - T + 1)$, as well as $Y(0)$, $Y(-1)$, $H(0)$, $H(-1)$, $U(0)$, $V(0)$, and $Z(0)$.

$H.$[5] The remaining variables are called *auxiliary* variables.

Six *fundamental equations* can be constructed, in which only the six fundamental variables appear as unknowns. Let us call this the *compressed* model.

The compressed model can also be solved recursively.[6] If $(T + G + 7)$ initial values were provided, the paths of the six fundamental variables would be uniquely determined for all time $t \geqq 1$.

It can be proved that, if the paths of the six fundamental variables have been uniquely determined using the compressed model, then – using this solution – the paths of all the auxiliary variables can also be determined uniquely. (With the exception of $p(t)$ and $X^*(t)$, the auxiliary variables are linearly dependent on the fundamental variables.)

Paths computed with the detailed and the compressed models are identical: the two models are equivalent. The advantage the compressed model offers is exactly as its name indicates: its compressed character. In most cases it is best to use it for analysing general mathematical properties of the model. Its disadvantage consists in its 'indigestibility' as far as economic interpretation is concerned.[7] As a result of compression, equations are exces-

---

[5] We have a certain freedom in selecting the six fundamental variables.

[6] The six fundamental variables are enumerated in the order in which they must be computed in the course of a recursive computation.

[7] It is worth mentioning at this point the order in which the two different forms of the model were developed. It was through 'compression' of the detailed model based on economic considerations that the compressed model came into being. (And not the other way round – that is, through disaggregating, according to economic criteria, the compressed model, which has a minimum size from the mathematical point of view.)

sively complicated and difficult to grasp. Therefore, we do not include them in this book. As a rule, we shall be using the detailed model and shall refer to the compressed form of the model only in a few formal propositions.

(5) The system follows a *feasible path*, if each of its variables assumes a non-negative value for each year $t \geqq 1$, and satisfies equations (A.1)–(A.11) describing the real sphere.

There exists a set of values for the real parameters that enables the system to move along a feasible path, along which production X(t) increases. (Appendix A explains what we mean by a *real* parameter.) A sufficient condition for the system to be able to grow is known to us, but we have not yet succeeded in finding the general form of the necessary and sufficient conditions.

I shall not present here the known sufficient condition. While its mathematical form is rather complicated, its economic content is trivial. A parameter constellation is needed that would guarantee that current inputs and household purchases together do not consume the entire production, but still leave some surplus for fixed capital investment and for increases in stocks. (The reader familiar with input–output analysis will certainly recognize the closeness of this condition to the well-known growth conditions for the dynamic Leontief economy.)

In the remainder of this book, it will be assumed that the real parameters of the model satisfy the above requirements; in other words, the system is *able to move along a feasible path and to grow*.

Normal path, Harrod–Neumann path

We shall begin with two definitions. The system follows

a *normal path*, if

$M(t) = M^*(t)$ (volume of investment inputs)

$X(t) = X^*(t)$ (production)

$Y(t) = Y^*(t)$ (firms' purchases)   (4.1)

$M(t) = M^*(t)$ (household purchases)

$W(t) = W^*(t)$ (real wage fund),

that is, if the actual value of each control variable equals its normal value, where the normal values are determined by the equations discussed earlier.

The system follows the *Harrod–Neumann path* (in short: the H–N path), if each of its reproducible stock and flow variables grows at a uniform and constant rate, that is, if

$M(t) = \Gamma^{*t} M_0$ (volume of investment vintage)

$X(t) = \Gamma^{*t} X_0$ (production)

$Y(t) = \Gamma^{*t} Y_0$ (firms' purchases)

$H(t) = \Gamma^{*t} H_0$ (household purchases)   (4.2)

$U(t) = \Gamma^{*t} U_0$ (output stocks)

$V(t) = \Gamma^{*t} V_0$ (input stocks)

in which $\Gamma^* > 1$ is the *general growth factor*, and the symbols with subscript 0 are the initial values (that is, values in year 0) of the variables in question.

The name derives from the fact that it was Harrod for aggregate models, and von Neumann for disaggregated ones, who developed the pioneering models whose most characteristic common feature is growth at a constant rate. As production and capital in Harrod's model, and as the production of all sectors in von Neumann's model grow at a uniform and constant rate, so, in the framework of the present model, all production, investment, trading and stock variables grow at a uniform and constant rate, when the system moves along the Harrod–Neumann path.

The following proposition can be made.

Given the assumptions of our model there exists a feasible normal path and this normal path is necessarily a Harrod–Neumann path. Apart from having real parameters which enable the system to grow on a feasible path, the following necessary and sufficient conditions must be satisfied to enable the system to have an H-N normal path:

(A) $\Gamma_M = \Gamma_Y = \Gamma_K = \Gamma_H = \Gamma_Z = \Gamma^*$,

(B) $\Psi = 1/\Phi$,   (4.3)

(C) $\Omega = \Psi$.

First of all, let us remark on the first two sentences of the above proposition. It is not self-evident that the normal path should be an H-N path. A well-defined normal path (where the actual and normal values of the control variables coincide) may exist in another model and with other assumptions, and that normal path might not be an H-N path. (For example, acceleration or deceleration might count as 'normal', or the normal growth rates of production, investment, trading and stock variables might not be uniform.) It is the *specific* property of our model that its normal path is an H-N path.

I shall add a few remarks on the conditions.

Condition (A). It is, of course, easy to understand that, if the general growth factor Γ^* appears uniformly in the determination of the normal values of the different control variables, this will allow the normal path to be an H–N path.[8] Despite that, the interrelation is not quite trivial.

There are quite a number of assumptions in our model which make it different from the Harrod and von Neumann models: the complicated lag structure, the vintage approach to investments, the use of input and output stocks, etc. It is reassuring that, notwithstanding these, we 'get back' the Harrod–Neumann results concerning steady growth.

There are altogether 10 equations determining the normal values of the variables (equations (A.17)–(A.26)). In five of them the growth factor is not even included: these equations deduce the normal value of some or other variable in another way; that is from direct economic relationships. (For example, the normal value of production follows from standard productivity and employment, the normal value of the real wage fund from the normal real wage and employment, and so on.) As for the remaining five equations, in three of them a growth factor is included, yet the normal value is determined in a certain sense endogenously: the *normal* value for year t equals the *actual* value for year $(t-1)$ multiplied by the growth factor. Therefore, these equations in themselves do not

[8] Because of the complicated lag structure in the model, no explicit formula can be given expressing the dependence of the general growth factor along the normal path on the parameters. Γ^* is implicitly determined by the characteristic polynomial of the system.

The uniqueness of the normal path has not been proved, nor do we know a set of conditions to ensure uniqueness.

We have worked out a numerical example, using Hungarian data and some approximated data. (The same collection of figures was used for the simulation presented later.) For these data $\Gamma^* = 1.06$, which is close to the average growth factor for Hungary in the 1960s.

exclude the possibility that, if the system left the H–N path one year, the normal value for the following year should also be outside the H–N path.

Only two normal values are 'imposed' exogenously on the H–N path. One is normal shortage represented by the variable $Z^*(t)$. The underlying economic assumption is the following: *normal shortage is in fact unchanged over time* when measured on the original scale, Z; multiplication by the growth factor Γ_Z^t, that is, the exogenous scaling up along the H–N path, was done just as a 'technical trick'.

The other variable similarly scaled up exogenously along the H–N path is the normal value of the investment vintage volume, that is $M^*(t)$. The underlying economic assumption is as follows: we wish to use our model to describe a system in which a *uniform rate of expansion of investment activity is regarded as normal. Ultimately, these two assumptions (normal shortage unchanged over time, constant rate of normal investment expansion) are embodied in the exogenously prescribed H–N paths of $Z^*(t)$ and $M^*(t)$. These two H–N paths then lead the many other normal variables in this growth model (and, under certain conditions, all of its reproducible stock and flow variables) along the Harrod–Neumann path.*

Condition (B). This condition expresses, in the language of our model, the fact that *technical progress is Harrod-neutral.*[9] This means that a unit of investment creates fewer jobs from vintage to vintage (Φ), and this is compen-

---

[9] On the Harrod-type neutrality of technical progress see, for example, the well-known survey of F. H. Hahn and R. C. O. Matthews, 'The theory of economic growth: a survey', *Economic Journal*, 74 (1964), 825–32. In Hungarian see R. Andorka, D. Dányi and B. Martos, *Dinamikus népgazdasági modellek* [Economy-wide dynamic models], Közgazdasági és Jogi Könyvkiadó, Budapest, 1967.

sated by the fact that productivity is higher for each newly created job than for the jobs created by earlier vintages (Ψ). Therefore, in the sense redefined in the model, the incremental 'output–capital ratio' is constant; more exactly: the ratio of the output–increment which can be produced by the investment vintage, to the estimated investment expenditure required to complete the investment vintage is constant over time.

Let us denote by $\Lambda_N(t)$ the *growth factor of employment*:

$$\Lambda_N(t) = N(t)/N(t - 1). \qquad (4.4)$$

$\Lambda_N(t)$ is not a parameter of the model, but it can be computed from the solution. The following relationships are satisfied along the normal path:

$$\Lambda_N(t) = \Lambda_N^* = \text{constant for every } t, \qquad (4.5)$$

$$\Gamma^* = \Lambda_N^* \Psi. \qquad (4.6)$$

Formula (4.6) is an expression of Harrod-neutrality, indicating that technical progress has a 'labour-augmenting' character. The factor Ψ scales up the growth of employment. On the normal path the growth of the reproducible stock and flow variables, Γ^*, is equal to the product of the growth factor of the non-reproducible resource, Λ (that is of the employed population), and that of productivity, Ψ.[10]

---

[10] For the sake of emphasis, the word 'productivity' was used somewhat imprecisely. In our model the growth factor of actual productivity:

$$\frac{X(t)/N(t)}{X(t - 1)/N(t - 1)}$$

may deviate from the growth factor for vintage productivity, Ψ. Along the normal path the two growth factors coincide.

ITHACA COLLEGE LIBRARY

Condition (C). The growth factor of the normal real wage rate must be equal to the growth factor of vintage productivity. This is necessary in order that along the normal path total household consumption should grow in accordance with the general growth factor.

5
Control and Stability

Controllability

On pages 68–74 the proposition was advanced that a feasible normal path exists in our system and that this path has Harrod–Neumann properties: along it, the reproducible stock and flow variables of the economy grow at a uniform and constant rate. Yet the structure of the model allows the system to move along other paths. *Whether or not the system follows the normal path depends on the control process.*

The model can be reformulated according to the standard terminology of mathematical control theory. For this purpose, we refer to the compressed form containing the six fundamental variables. These include three *state variables*: the output stock $U(t)$, the input stock $V(t)$, and the deviation of actual shortage from its normal level, $\hat{Z}(t)$. There are also three *control variables*: the volume of the investment vintage $M(t)$, firms' purchases $Y(t)$, and household purchases $H(t)$. In accordance with this classification of variables, the compressed model of six equations comprises three state equations and three control equations.

We can then put forward the following proposition: *the system of state equations is controllable.*

The concept of 'controllability' is well known in mathematical control theory.[1] It means that whatever state the system is in, there is a path for the control variables which drives the system to any assigned feasible state within a finite time period. Such an assigned state could be an appropriate point along the normal path. In this case *controllability means that, if the system departs from its normal path, a suitable choice of the control variables can help to drive it back to the normal path within a finite period.*

Endogenous description of the control

A considerable volume of literature on growth theory deals with the question of control, yet in most cases the analysis is conducted 'outside the model'. Questions such as the effects of prices, nominal wages or interest rate signals, or the equilibrating mechanisms that might be functioning, etc., are often touched on, without, however, being formally incorporated into the model itself.

Let us consider, for example, the von Neumann model. As a result of some analysis, we can determine the optimum prices and the interest rate associated with the real path that guarantees the fastest growth. However, these are not 'fed back' into the model: they do not act as feedback signals.

The present model tries to take a step forward in this respect. *As it evolves over time, the system itself generates signals which, 'fed back' into the same system, will influence its subsequent development.*

---

[1] See, for example, D. G. Luenberger, *Introduction to Dynamic Systems*, Wiley, New York, 1979; or A. E. Bryson and Yu-Chi Ho, *Applied Optimal Control*, Ginn, Waltham, 1969.

Let us turn to Appendix A, where the equations are grouped according to the following important criterion: equations (A.1)–(A.11): the *real sphere* of the system; equations (A.12)–(A.26): the *control sphere* of the system.

Among the most important properties of the growth model described in this study is that it represents the control sphere *in even more detail* (15 equations), than it represents the real sphere (11 equations).

I should not be immodest. I do not claim that this is a really *good* model of control in a socialist economy. I readily admit that the description is rough and simple. If it has any merits, it is rather the undertaking itself: *to build a growth model with endogenous control of real process*; and in such a way as to model the interactions between long- and short-term control.

Nor do I claim that this is the only or even the first attempt of its kind,[2] though we can be sure that it is still quite rare, despite the desirability of intensifying research along these lines.

Control by norms

The model presents a specific form of control, which we call *control by norms*. (The expression 'norm' and

[2] I should mention here András Bródy's new book: *Ciklus és szabályozás* [Cycle and Control], Közgazdasági és Jogi Könyvkiadó, Budapest, 1980. It constructs a model of a special type of endogenous control for a dynamic Leontief economy. From the same point of view M. Lackó's previously mentioned investment control model is also remarkable, as is E. A. Hewett's study which incorporates the planners' response functions as endogenous control into an econometric model of the Hungarian economy. (See 'A Macroeconometric Model of a Centrally Planned Economy with Endogenous Plans: The Hungarian Case' (mimeographed), University of Texas, Austin, 1980.)

'normal value' are considered synonyms.) Its theoretical basis and mathematical background were discussed in detail in the book *Non-Price Control* mentioned previously; we can only add a few words about it here.

Let us denote by $u(t)$ the vector of control variables in the model, and by $x(t)$ the vector of state variables. Symbols with an asterisk indicate normal values of the same variables. Let us now examine the structure of the control sphere using this notation.

Equations (A.12)–(A.16) describe the *determination of the control variables*. They have the following general form:

$$u(t) - u^*(t) =$$
$$f_1(x(t) - x^*(t), u(t-1) - u^*(t-1), \ldots,$$
$$u(t - G) - u^*(t - G)). \qquad (5.1)$$

The current value of each control variable deviates from its normal value if the current value of the associated state variables deviates from its normal value, and/or if previous values of that control variables deviated from their normal values in earlier periods.

Equations (A.17)–(A.26) describe the *generation of normal values.* (With two exceptions, these are generated endogenously.) This part of the system of equations is divided into two blocks. Equations (A.17)–(A.21) and (A.24–A.25) determine the *normal values of the control variables*:

$$u^*(t) = f_2(u(t - 1), \ldots, u(t - G - T)), \qquad (5.2)$$

while equations (A.22)–(A.23) determine the *normal values of the state variables*:

$$x^*(t) = f_3(u(t - 1), \ldots, u(t - G)). \qquad (5.3)$$

This kind of relationship between the variables u, x, u^* and x^* (including the specification of the lag structure) is an accidental specific property of our model. A number of other variations are conceivable, and in constructing another model it may well be justified to employ assumptions different from those used in this study.

Studying the norms gives us a profound insight into the nature of the system. If we really know what is regarded as 'normal' in a system, we know quite a lot about that system.

Norms are fixed by habit, convention, tacit or legally supported social acceptance, or conformity. They tend to perpetuate themselves, and the longer they are valid, the more deeply rooted they become; the inertia of society then ensures their effectiveness over an extended period.

Our working hypothesis is as follows: *in a given historical period social norms are unchanged over time.* Of course, this does not mean that they are, in the mathematical sense, uniquely defined. If they appear in the model as uniquely determined constants, this is only for the convenience of model construction. In practice, we ought to formalize them rather as intervals or as means of probability distributions.

Norms are not fixed for ever, and sometimes they can change rather dramatically. If that happens, it indicates a transition to a qualitatively different period, or, to another 'regime'. The logic can also be reversed: the constancy of the most important norms can be regarded as a basic criterion for periodizing history for constructing the typology of difference 'regimes'.

In this approach to social phenomena, we do *not* ask what is useful, what is desirable, or what is optimal. We merely enquire about what *exists*. What is normal, 'regular', and 'natural' about this system? This is the typical way of formulating a question in a descriptive-explanatory theory.

One of the attractions of this approach is that it suggests obvious possibilities for testing the theory empirically. Norms can be recognized, first of all by observing the means and trends exhibited by time series and cross-section data on various recurrent phenomena or on phenomena occurring in a number of different places.

Of course, not all mean values should be regarded as norms. *A mean is justifiably treated as a norm only if there exists some control mechanism that drives the actual value of the variable toward its normal value.* This idea introduces us to the subject of the next section; namely the stability of control.

With reference to our remarks on pp. 76–80 I shall digress here briefly in order to comment on the role of *central economic policy and planning*. As I stressed earlier, the model presents the *joint outcomes* of decision processes taking place at all the upper and lower levels of control, and does not separate the influence of the centre from that of lower-level decision-makers. As for the resulting joint effect itself, the model describes it in a deterministic framework. The control process responds to the impulses affecting it by applying certain 'rules of the game'. Reality, of course, is much more complicated than that. First, the effect exerted by the centre does not directly merge with the other components of control; its role is exceedingly important and responsible. Secondly, neither the centre, nor the lower-level decision-makers are mere executors of given rules, since they all have some scope for choice. Although I am fully aware of all this, these observations 'do not fit' in the present mathematical model. Whatever formulation we adopt, it may, on the one hand, be a workable instrument in the researcher's hands, and on the other hand, it may turn out to be a strait-jacket for the very same researcher. It can both assist and inhibit analysis all at once.

The formulation chosen here can be used at most for an indirect examination of certain features of behaviour in the fields of economic policy and planning. (For example, certain types of behaviour can be described by various collections of exogenous parameters: rapid or reluctant, calm or hysterical reaction, and so on.) If, however, we wish to study more comprehensively the independent role and alternative forms of behaviour of the central economic policy-makers and of the central planners, then it would be necessary to construct a different model.

Examination of stability

In this section we shall employ the concept of *stability* solely in the sense in which it is used in the *mathematical* theory of dynamic systems, following Lyapunov and others.[3] We shall, therefore, depart from the usage of economists dealing with business cycles and prices, who would certainly regard a system that followed a widely fluctuating path as 'unstable', even though, for the mathematician, it might be 'stable' in the sense of converging to the equilibrium path.

Although the concept is borrowed from the mathematician's vocabulary, stability in this sense is also of great importance for theoretical economics. In the framework of the model *an examination of stability answers the following question: do the control rules and behavioural regulari-*

---

[3] For the definitions of various types of stability see for example Luenberger's *Introduction to Dynamic Systems*, p. 332. In our own stability investigations we applied, as a rule, the criterion of asymptotic stability.

ties formulated in the model guarantee that the system, having once departed from the normal path, will eventually return to it or approach it? If the answer is negative, it is doubtful whether there is any sense at all in talking about norms, normal values, or a normal path. If the answer is positive, and the system is stable in a wider or a narrower sense, the use of these categories is both sensible and justified. Then – and only then – can we say that the norms *are asserted.* The actual path is close to the normal path, fluctuates around it and cannot completely break away from it.

If we already have some understanding of stability conditions, it is also useful for us to know what can cause *instability.* For example, what constellations of parameters lead the system, once it leaves the normal path, never to return to it?

After these introductory remarks, let us now examine the stability of our own model. The difficulty of making precise statements about the stability of 'imperfectly behaved' multivariable dynamic systems is well known. It is no wonder if, in the present model, we can only provide a few propositions of limited validity and set forth certain conjectures.

Let us start with a definition. The system is controlled *without feedback*, if, on the right-hand sides of the control equations (A.12)–(A.16) only the normal value associated with the variable to be controlled has a non-zero coefficient, that is, $M^*(t)$ in the equation controlling $M(t)$, $X^*(t)$ in the equation controlling $X(t)$, and so on. In this block of equations the coefficients of all the other explanatory variables are zero:

$$\mu_H = \mu_K = \mu_Z = \xi_U = \xi_Z = \eta_V = \eta_Z = \chi_Z = \omega_H = 0. \quad (5.4)$$

The coefficients listed above are called *feedback para-*

meters. If at least one of them is non-zero, we can talk about *feedback* control.

Necessary and sufficient conditions for local asymptotic stability of the control without feedback can be determined mathematically.[4]

I shall not elaborate on these conditions, since for most of them no clear economic interpretation can be given.[5] The proposition itself cannot satisfy an economist, since what interests us most is precisely the effect of feedback.

Before proceeding to further conclusions, we must again introduce a new concept. Feedback is said to *improve* control if either of the effects (A) and (B) set out below is operative.

Effect (A). The real parameters provide for local asymptotic stability without feedback. With the introduction of suitable feedback this type of stability remains and *convergence is accelerated*. If, for example, something causes the system to depart from its normal path, it will return to it more quickly with feedback than without it.

Effect (B). Real parameters without feedback do not ensure stability. Yet the *introduction of suitable feedback renders the system locally asymptotically stable*.

We can put forward our conjecture: *there exists a collection of feedback parameters – all nine elements of which*

[4] The attribute 'local' indicates that the system must start not too far from the normal path to be able to approach it asymptotically.

[5] I shall mention just one, which has a clear economic meaning. Equation (A.11) explaining shortage contains the real parameter ζ_Z which expresses the autoregressive effect of shortage. One of the necessary conditions for asymptotic stability is $\zeta_Z < 1$, in other words, that the self-generating effect of shortage should diminish over time. If $\zeta_Z > 1$, shortage would intensify and the system would move further and further away from normal shortage.

are positive and of a magnitude that can be economically interpreted – which improves control in the sense defined above.

We have called this a conjecture rather than a proposition, since we have no general mathematical proof of the assertion. At present, we can only provide some indirect support. The most obvious means of examining the stability of multivariable dynamic systems – given our inability to obtain more complete results at the level of pure theory – is *computer simulation*. This is what we did and the results proved to be quite reassuring.

One of the most typical results of the simulation is summarized in Figure 11. We carried out a series of computations, with identical parameters throughout.[6] Without feedback, this system turned out to be unstable. We wished to find out to what extent the system would be stabilized through the introduction of feedback. For the purposes of this explanation let us denote by h the vector of the nine feedback parameters. The following formula was used: $h = s \cdot g$, in which g is an initially chosen vector of feedback parameters, and s is a scalar, which assumed, successively, the values 0.1, 0.2, ..., 1, 1.1, ... Accordingly, s measures in the simplest possible form the *'strength' of the feedback*. This scalar s is measured along the horizontal axis of the figure.

The initial values of the variables are generally on their normal paths. In each run the initial value of only one variable is made to move off the normal path. Three

---

[6] These real parameters should be regarded as a 'stylized' illustration of Hungary's economic characteristics. Where time-series were available in Hungarian economic statistics, estimates were based on them; this was usually done by means of a trend calculation. Other estimates could only be supported by statistical data indirectly. Besides, there were quite a few parameters for which the estimation had to be done arbitrarily, relying only on our 'economist's instinct'.

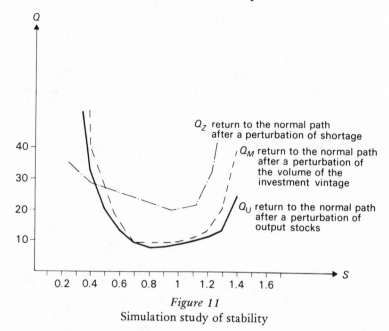

Figure 11
Simulation study of stability

different perturbations were tried, with output stock, investment vintage volume, or shortage deviating from the corresponding normal value. The indicator Q on the vertical axis shows the number of periods the perturbed system requires to return to a neighbourhood of the normal path. The three curves on the figure correspond to the three different perturbations.

The figure shows clearly the stabilizing effect of feedback. It also suggests that, at least for this extremely simplified computation, feedback has a certain most effective strength (about 0.9 in our example), at which convergence is fastest. If feedback is too weak or insensitive convergence is very slow (or does not take place at all), and the situation is similar if it is too strong or abrupt. Of course, from this small-scale experiment involving severe *ceteris paribus* restrictions, it is impossible to draw far-reaching conclusions about the 'optimum feedback strength'.[7] Yet the experiment does lend some support to the conjecture underlined above, according to which feedback improves control, and stabilizes an otherwise unstable system.

The conjecture is further supported by an investigation covering control not of the whole model, but of a certain section of it. Non-zero feedback parameters are specified only in the control equations for *short-term* variables: production X, the firms' purchases Y, and household purchases H (and in these equations only in relation to the shortage reactions). As opposed to this, no feedback is allowed in the control equations for *long-term* variables, including in that for the investment vintage volume M. Instead, these variables are 'forced' on to their normal paths. In that case it can be proved mathematically that the system can be locally asymptotically stabilized, and that necessary and sufficient conditions for stability can be determined. This result suggests interesting possibilities for analysis; thus, among other things, it may facilitate an investigation of the relationship between short- and long-term control.

The stability properties of the model are worth further study, with both analytical and simulation methods. In any case, from the stability point of view, nothing can be

[7] Prudence in drawing conclusions is also justified because the same short series of simulation results suggests that the system is sensitive to perturbations; it is easily shifted from its normal path and only returns to it slowly.

Otherwise, a better constellation of the feedback parameters may accelerate convergence. For example, with $s = 0.9$ we concentrated on adjusting the feedback parameters in the investment control equation. In this way we succeeded in shortening considerably the return time Q_M.

said that prevents us from using the model. The concepts of 'norm', and 'normality' can be interpreted within the framework of the model, since the control mechanisms built into it are – at least for suitable parameter values – able to keep the motion of the system in the neighbourhood of its own norms.[8]

Finally, an additional remark on methodology. In economic applications of mathematical control theory the following line of thought is usually pursued:

The description of a real sphere is given. Furthermore, the sets of economic policy targets and instruments are also given. The question is then to determine the control rules that best serve the given economic policy objectives. The control equations of the model are not specified in advance, but their determination is exactly the *result* of the research. Accordingly, it is unnecessary to ask whether the control has such desirable properties as stability, rapid convergence, etc. Of course it has, since the researcher was seeking a control for which he postulated in advance that it should have these properties.

This is the *normative* approach to the modelling of economic control. Yet we wish to develop a *descriptive* approach, in which the corresponding train of thought goes as follows:

---

[8] A word of warning seems useful at this point. The present system describes a *self-repeating routine* form of control. Stability of the system amounts to saying, for this model, that if conditions remain unchanged, the economy's control mechanism can perpetuate the *status quo*.

The chosen formulation does not seem to be suitable for representing endogenously (i.e. within the model) the ways in which adaptation to sudden changes in external conditions takes place, or how a new historical era begins, which entails the development of new norms and new behavioural regularities. This is *another subject*, and a completely different type of economic theory and mathematics would be needed for its investigation.

We observe in reality and seek to describe in the model not only the real sphere but also the control sphere. The model of the latter must reflect – in more or less detail – the way in which control takes place in reality. What are the decision rules, and how and to what signals do the decision-makers react?

Thus we build into the model some equations reflecting to some degree the empirically observable control mechanism, and *then* ask how the system functions and study it stability properties.

We did not put the rabbit in the top hat beforehand just to be able to pull it out triumphantly afterwards. We did not construct a control block knowing in advance that it could ensure stability. In the circumstances, therefore, our stability results must be considered all the more valuable.

Normal path: non-Walrasian long-term equilibrium

We begin with a terminological question. Let us suppose that this model gets into the hands of a 'pure' mathematician unsullied by economics, someone who specializes in the mathematical theory of dynamic systems. He would certainly call the normal path an equilibrium path.

About this question, complete terminological confusion prevails among economists. Some economists regard every state – or, in the case of a dynamic model, every path – of the system which is characterized by non-Walrasian properties as a *dis*equilibrium state.[9] This implies that the only

---

[9] See for example the works of Barro, Grossmann, and a number of other authors belonging to the 'disequilibrium school'. The title of one of the articles – important also for its content – is quite typical: 'On persistent disequilibrium' (H. R. Varian, *Journal of Economic Theory*, 12 (1975), 218–28). In my earlier book, *Anti-Equilibrium*, my usage was similar in this respect.

genuine equilibrium is the Walrasian equilibrium; any system deviating from it – even if such deviations are permanent and persistent – is not in equilibrium.

Other economists are, however, prepared to talk about a non-Walrasian equilibrium. They use, for example, the expression 'Keynesian unemployment equilibrium', etc. The use of the term 'non-Walrasian equilibrium' seems to be taking root, particularly among Western theoretical economists, though it cannot yet be considered to be generally accepted.

As for myself, I accept the second definition. In my view it is, though different from the traditional interpretation of equilibrium in economics, in harmony with the concept of equilibrium in mathematics, and in the natural sciences. Within the scope of our model, the terms *'normal path' and 'non-Walrasian long-term equilibrium' are synonyms.* Nevertheless, although I have no theoretical objection against using the *word* in such a broad, 'natural scientific' interpretation, I refrain from using it on practical grounds, and prefer the terms 'normal state' and 'normal path'. These terms, not having any particular economic past, seem more advantageous, since they are less likely to cause misunderstanding in the existing terminological confusion. Being a Hungarian economist, it is also reasonable for me to take into account the terminology that has come to be accepted throughout my country. Hungarian economists would, almost without exception, and without referring to Walras, call shortage *dis*equilibrium, though all of them know that shortage is always with us and has been continuously reproduced for several decades. This consideration also makes me hesitate to use an expression like 'shortage equilibrium' (the counterpart of 'Keynesian unemployment equilibrium'). It has to be recognized that value-judgements are bound to be associated with the concept of equilibrium: equilibrium is 'good', disequilibrium 'bad' in the eyes of most people, within or outside the profession. On the other hand, the terms 'normal state' or 'normal path' seem to be free of any value-judgement; that is, neutral.

I shall now point out the non-Walrasian properties of the system represented in our growth model.

(1) *Constant reproduction of shortage*. We should not expect to find a primary explanation of this fact in the behaviour of the household sector whose demands are constrained by the wage fund W. The principal explanation lies in the behaviour of the firms' sector, particularly on the demand side. The firms' decision-makers, and those governing the firms' sector at higher levels of economic management, are constantly influenced by the expansion drive which generates an almost insatiable investment hunger. Because of shortage there is a widespread hoarding tendency, which is one of the main reasons why the demand of the firms' sector is almost insatiable. There are no financial and profitability considerations to restrain effectively the firms' exaggerated demand. A vicious circle is thus created: shortage → quantity drive → increased demand for inputs → increasingly intensive shortage → . . .

At the same time, counter-forces operate to drive the system back to the normal level of shortage. Unusually intensive shortage dampens down the purchasing intensions of firms and puts a brake on investment starts.

The behaviour of the firms' sector is system-specific, as described here in the control equations determining the variables M, X, and Y. This behaviour differs essentially from that of capitalist firms.

(2) *Non-Walrasian signal system*. In our model the actual values of the control variables depart from their normal values through the effects of various *non-price signals*. The most important of these include stock signals,

shortage signals, and changes in the investment commitment and household consumption.

Given the nature of these models, these signals are represented by *macro*-variables. In fact, however, they represent
collections of millions of microsignals. $V < V^*$ means that
input stocks have diminished in hundreds of factory warehouses; $Z > Z^*$ means that queues are longer, and forced
substitutions more frequent than normal; $H < H^*_{plan}$ means
that there are more complaints about living standards
among the population, and so on.

In recent years it has become increasingly clear to
theoretical economists that non-price signals play an
important role in economic systems. The present model
tries to take a step forward by formalizing, in the framework of a macro-model, the generation of non-price signals
and their 'feedback' as part of the decision control process.

Given the non-Walrasian character of the system, it is
appropriate to comment on Malinvaud's Helsinki
lectures. It is an intellectually attractive experiment to
present different 'regimes' on the same diagram, as different
points in a given co-ordinate system, or as definite regions
of the co-ordinate plane. Malinvaud identifies in his
diagrams points or areas corresponding to Walrasian equilibrium, Keynesian and 'classical' unemployment, etc. I was
tempted to locate in these diagrams the economy I am
examining. Should it not be the regime that Malinvaud
calls 'repressed inflation'?

In my view, this would not be correct. *A semi-monetized
economy in which prices and money do not genuinely
influence the macrovariables of production, investment,
and employment cannot properly be described in terms of
its money being stable or inflated, or price increases being
repressed or permitted.* The main characteristic features of
this system summarized above – chronic shortage, strong

expansion drive, quantity drive, unrestrainable investment spirit – can be observed when the price level is stable. But they would also persist if the price level began to change and a slow or accelerating inflation evolved.

The system I am investigating cannot be modelled merely by substituting different numerical parameters into Malinvaud's equations. We must instead provide other equations, in which other behavioural regularities, other signal systems, and other feedback mechanisms are formulated.

The present study does not attempt to judge, whether the model of Barro, Grossman and Malinvaud offers an appropriate way of distinguishing between alternative states of a capitalist economy, that is, for developing a typology of capitalist 'regimes' differing from each other in certain essential features. It seems certain, however, that the description of a socialist economy can hardly be pressed into the same theoretical framework.

6

Efficiency and Employment

The model described in the preceding chapters can be used to carry out several different types of analysis. In the present study we shall use it, as an illustration, to examine a single group of questions, to do with efficiency. Even in this field, we do not exhaust the possibilities of analysis offered by the model.

Efficiency is a composite and multidimensional concept. Accordingly, we shall only discuss a few aspects of it without trying to be complete.

Efficiency of consumption

This is an unusual concept,[1] yet its interpretation is facilitated by our model. Along the normal path of the economy two different processes take place simultaneously:

$$H(t) = H^*(t) = \Gamma^* H(t - 1), \qquad (6.1)$$

---

[1] I borrowed this term from the eminent Czechoslovak economist J. Goldmann. (See *Macroekonomická analyza a prognóza*, Academia, Praha, 1975.)

that is, real household consumption grows at a constant rate, and

$$Z(t) = Z^*(t), \qquad (6.2)$$

that is, normal shortage is constantly reproduced. This is consistent with several shortage phenomena that affect the household: certain consumer articles are not on sale at all, while others are only available in a limited selection. Purchases cause the buyer a great deal of trouble. He goes from one shop to the next until he finds either the desired article or an acceptable forced substitute. He often has to join a queue. Real queues are formed for articles of small value in certain shops, and the buyer might have to wait for hours. For products or services of higher value (such as a car, or a flat) symbolic, 'numbered' queues are formed, in which the waiting time may be several years.

The two different types of phenomena are frequently confused. Many consider shortage as a symptom of poverty and a low level of economic development. And yet the question is actually about two clearly distinguishable processes. Consumption may be low, while there is no 'shortage' in the sense that the buyer can spend the money he has on what he wants, with nothing on the supply side preventing this. On the other hand, chronic shortage may arise at high or low per capita consumption levels or, in conjunction with relatively slow or relatively rapid growth rates of consumption.

Let us compare two countries A and B, in which – to simplify the comparison – per capita real household consumption levels are identical. If, however, shortage intensity is higher (measured by an indicator suitable for making comparisons between the countries) in country A than in country B, *consumption must be less efficient in the former, because the acquisition of an identical volume of products is accompanied by more trouble, annoyance, and disappointment.* I do not see much sense in constructing a composite welfare function for comparisons of this kind, having both consumption and shortage as arguments: instead, it seems much more important to understand the *causal* linkage.

Thus the *same* economic growth-patterns and, along with this, the same economic mechanism that are able continuously to increase real consumption levels, simultanously reproduce shortage phenomena within the sphere of consumption.

After these few remarks on the efficiency of *consumption* let us now turn our attention, in more detail, to an examination of the efficiency of *production.*

Input–output proportions and shortage

Let us first consider the resources already *drawn into* the production process, and ask what happens to their utilization. (Later on, we shall also ask what happens to the resources *not drawn into* production, including the most important one: able-bodied but unemployed people.)

Our first example concerns the connection between current inputs and shortage, which is shown in Figure 12. (We examined the situation at a given moment of time, so that the argument t can be omitted.) We shall analyse initially not our model but the actual practice of a shortage economy.

The ratio $\tilde{\alpha} = A/X$ is an increasing convex function of shortage; it rises increasingly steeply as shortage becomes more intensive. A similar relationship holds for investment inputs and labour inputs. For the sake of uniformity let us

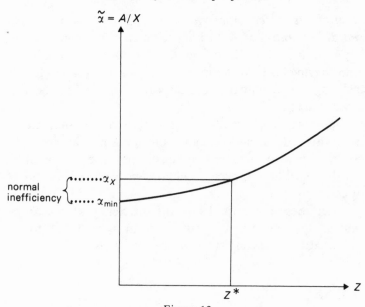

Figure 12
Current input coefficient as a function of shortage

introduce the corresponding notation, $\tilde{\beta} = B/X$ and $\tilde{\gamma} = N/X$.[2]

Although the interdependence between shortage and inputs into production was mentioned when the equations were first set out, we wish to illuminate the matter more fully now. In the paragraphs that follow shortage is always the *cause* and inefficiency the *effect*.[3]

---

[2] For the sake of uniformity, we chose to write down here the reciprocal of productivity. For the relationships between N/X and p or q see p. 60.

[3] In the situations to be listed what Leibenstein calls 'allocative inefficiency' and 'X-inefficiency' are intertwined, but with the emphasis more on the latter.

(1) Shortage leads to interruptions to production: some worker or perhaps an entire workshop or section of a plant must *stand idle*, because one or more essential inputs are not available. This primarily affects $\tilde{\gamma}$.

(2) Shortage leads to *forced substitutions*. The lacking inputs have to be replaced with something inferior or more expensive, whether this is some material, a semi-finished product, a spare part, a machine, a piece of equipment, a certain type of performance, etc. This directly affects all three input–output proportions adversely.

(3) Disorganization resulting from shortage *undermines the discipline and morale of labour*. Chronic labour shortage has a similar effect (we shall soon discuss this in more detail), making it more difficult for managers to take effective action against workers violating factory discipline. Shortage phenomena affecting household supplies can weaken the population's enthusiasm for labour. All this promotes the growth of $\tilde{\gamma}$, while it also affects the other two input–output proportions.

(4) The natural counterpart of shortage is, as already stressed, the *quantity drive*. Buyers press for delivery as rapidly as possible of the largest possible quantity. This one-sided effort to increase quantity discourages firms from economizing on inputs and taking care about the quality of the resulting output.

(5) In the above paragraphs examples were cited showing that shortage can, in the short term, be a direct cause of inefficiency. However, there is also an indirect interrelation operating over the longer-term and this may be even more important. In a chronic shortage economy the producer only experiences problems in selling his goods exceptionally and temporarily. The 'seller's market' provides protection for those producing at high cost, and for those conserving inefficiently old technologies or producing according to traditional product patterns.

The relationships referred to above take effect through a million elementary events: each actual shortage phenomenon leads to a certain deterioration in efficiency. These, however, are not isolated events; rather they are linked together by innumerable ties, spilling over and amplifying one another.

In the model the causal linkages between shortage and inefficiency are represented, of course, in a severely simplified way. The huge number of elementary events is represented by a few macro-variables. Since the three different input–output proportions are so closely interdependent, we are justified in supposing that they are all affected by the same variable Z. The strictly convex (and in the case of productivity, strictly concave) functions are replaced by approximations linearized about the value of Z^* corresponding to normal shortage.

The input parameters include from the outset a certain degree of *normal inefficiency*. For the ratio α_X this was also shown in Figure 12. The minimum ratio A/X attainable in a state completely free from shortage was denoted by $\alpha_{\min}$. The normal inefficiency occurring with normal shortage is given by the difference $(\alpha_X - \alpha_{\min})$. Of course, if shortage is more intensive than normal, inefficiency increases further.

With a view to ensuring the mathematical tractability of the model, we are compelled to disregard a number of other effects of shortage, not reflected in the quantities $\tilde{\alpha}$, $\tilde{\beta}$ and $\tilde{\gamma}$, that also tend to lower efficiency. Thus, among other things, we disregard the fact that the stock norms ρ and σ, the gestation period G and the economic life of fixed capital T (in other words, the rate of scrapping) all depend both on the normal and the instantaneous actual intensity of shortage. Instead, we treat all these magnitudes as exogenous constants in the model. Still, even though the representation is simple and rough, the connec-

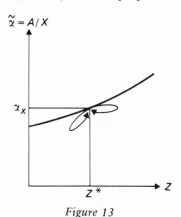

Figure 13
The system is stable: input returns to the normal path

tion between shortage and efficiency is at least to some
extent brought out. In this respect our model is rather
exceptional in the literature on macroeconomics and
growth; usually, input–output proportions do not vary
with the general state of the market, or with macroeconomic indicators of excess demand, excess supply,
shortage and slack in such models.

If the system is stable, input–output proportions fluc-
tuate about their own normal levels. This is illustrated with
the example of A/X in Figure 13, but of course, it is also
valid for the other two ratios. Yet the control of the
system may turn out to be unstable — and not only in the
model, but in practice as well. In such cases, a vicious
circle can arise, in which shortage at an intensity higher
than normal lowers efficiency, this lower efficiency then
leads to an intensification of shortage which further
reduces efficiency and so on; and all this can continue
without the system returning to its original normal path.
Perhaps new norms may become established at less advantageous levels: Z^* might be substituted by Z^{**}, and α_X by
α'_X (see Figure 14).

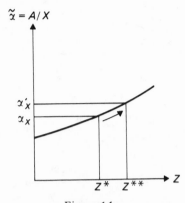

Figure 14
The system is unstable: input does not return to the normal path

Let us now revert to the case we are examining closely, in which the control of the system is stable and the norms are given. We can then conclude that *as long as the normal shortage persists in the system, this kind of inefficiency (expressed in the input–output proportions) will also persist.* I do not claim that shortage is the only factor that can reduce efficiency. Nevertheless, with its direct and indirect effects combined it is one of the most important factors, which provides some justification for assigning it such a leading role in the model.

In a rather simple form, the model thus expresses what we might call *the efficiency paradox of the shortage economy.* On the one hand, shortage as a *signal* or *impulse*, stimulates *increases* in production. In our model this effect is represented by equation (A.13), especially by the feedback parameters ξ_U and ξ_Z. On the other hand, the *real effects* of shortage tend to reduce efficiency – as already explained – and thereby *impede* production.

The relationship is illustrated in Figure 15, on the basis of a simulation exercise. The system was initially moving along its normal path and was then perturbed: actual

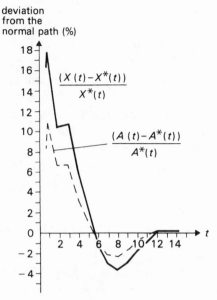

Figure 15
Simulation of the 'efficiency paradox'

shortage in a given year then exceeded the normal level by 20 per cent. This shortage signal triggered off the quantity drive: actual production suddenly increases and considerably exceeds its normal level. At the same time, inputs depart from their normal levels. Sooner or later, however, production (and inputs) slow down and fall below the normal path. In the end, with gradually diminishing amplitude, the system returns to the normal path.

The efficiency paradox is manifest in that an apparent contradiction exists between micro- and macro-level observations. At the *micro*-level the shop manager says he cannot produce more under the given conditions. The intention to increase production comes up against one bottleneck after another. The resource which constitutes the bottleneck at any particular time and place is fully exploited. At the same time, *macro*-level data reveal that, for large aggregates and over long periods, the average utilization ratio is rather low. (For illustration, we present some data on the level of stocks and the utilization of machines in Tables B.5 and B.6 of Appendix B.)

Yet those who have thoroughly understood the nature of chronic shortage and the efficiency paradox of the shortage economy will not see any logical contradiction between these micro- and macro-level observations, and can even claim that they are, in a sense, preconditions for each other.

The extensive period: absorption of reserve labour

After discussing in the preceding section the utilization of the *active* resources drawn into the production process, we shall now turn our attention to another aspect of efficiency, by enquiring how far the system succeeds in *activating* its available resources. To what extent has it drawn them into the production process, and what proportion of them remains inactive outside the production process? This question could be raised in respect of land, minerals, or any other natural resources; but in this book we concentrate attention on one particular resource, namely *labour*.

Eastern-European countries were at a low or medium development level when they assembled at the starting line to undertake growth in socialist conditions. At that time a high rate of open or hidden unemployment and under-employment was characteristic of agricultural regions; and the level of employment of women was relatively low.

I shall now put forward a proposition that follows from the present model (and from the general theory underlying it) and which is confirmed by *Eastern-European economic experience* since the Second World War.

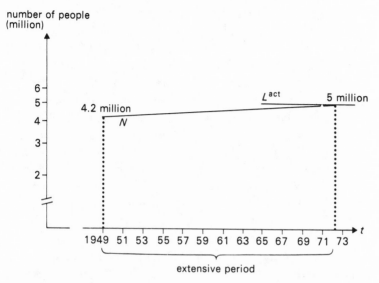

Figure 16
Absorption of labour reserves (Hungarian data)

The type of economic growth represented in our model (with given demographic conditions) is bound to lead to the absorption of reserve labour, to full employment and to a high activity rate of the population.

Let us begin the argument for this proposition with an illustration from Hungary's economic history. Figure 16 is based on Hungarian statistical data and computations carried out with the model which used Hungarian data. The horizontal axis shows historical time. We took 1949 as the starting point, this being the year before the start of Hungary's first 5-year-plan. By that time postwar reconstruction was complete and large-scale nationalization had already taken place: that year is reasonably considered the start of socialist-type growth.

We measure labour on the vertical axis, using a logarithmic scale.

$N(1949)$ that is, employment at the start, was 4.2 million people. The yearly average growth rate of employment was 0.7 per cent up to 1972, that is to say, $\Lambda_N = 1.007$.

To clarify the supply side let us introduce a new concept: that of *the potentially active population*. It can be interpreted most easily by starting from its opposite. Part of the population of working age is practically unemployable, for health, family, or other social reasons. The rest is potentially active. In other words: the size of the potentially active population represents the upper limit to labour supply. Various external conditions may lead labour supply to be less than this, but it cannot be more. Now, as for the Hungarian data, these show that the growth of population is very slow. We shall not fall into serious error if we take the ratio of the potentially active population to the population of working age as a constant. Accordingly, let us consider the size of the potentially active population as constant: 5 million.[4] It will be denoted by L^{act}.

The two curves N and L^{act} intersect. Let us stop there – the more recent period is discussed later on.

Of course, the figure shows the course of development in a very simplified manner. The growth of employment did not take place quite so smoothly, though the time series of the actual data do not deviate too much from the exponential trend shown in the figure. It is obvious also that the growth trend of employment does not come up against very severe supply constraints. There had been all along a partial labour shortage, just as there has been some reserve labour since 1972, and it is even reproduced. And yet Hungarian experts on labour economics agree that it

---

[4] It is, in fact, not very important how we define and measure the potentially active population for the period before 1972. The exact limits only become important when labour reserves have been exhausted.

was around 1972–73 when a qualitative change took place in the labour market situation.

In the terminology now accepted in Eastern Europe the period when there is enough potentially active reserve labour and this reserve is being gradually absorbed is called the *extensive period*. The *intensive period* is characterized by full employment, and the absence of any substantial potentially active labour reserves. Thus the extensive period ended in Hungary around 1972.

Now let us describe, using the conceptual apparatus of the model, the interrelations determining employment in the extensive period.

$$\Gamma^*\Phi = \Lambda_D^* = \Lambda_N^*. \qquad (6.3)$$

From left to right, this formula indicates the direction of *causal linkages*.

Expansion drive and investment hunger working within the system result in persistent forceful growth. With given real parameters the economy moves along its normal path according to the general growth factor Γ^*. Technical progress has a labour-saving quality even during that period ($\Phi < 1$), though the shift towards labour-saving techniques is not particularly rapid. (In the model we estimated $\Phi = 0.953$ for the Hungarian extensive period.) The product $\Gamma^*\Phi$ determines the growth factor for labour *demand*: Λ_D^*. While there are sufficient labour reserves, labour demand can be satisfied, so that employment can increase according to the same growth factor, Λ_N^*.

To ensure that the extensive period is finite, the following condition must be satisfied:

$$\Lambda_D^* > \Lambda^{\text{act}*}, \qquad (6.4)$$

in which $\Lambda^{\text{act}*}$ is the growth factor of the potentially active population. In Hungary the above condition was in fact satisfied, with $\Lambda_D^* = 1.007$, $\Lambda^{act*} \approx 1$. This ensured that the extensive period could not last much more than 20 years.

Condition (6.4) incorporates, as a matter of fact, a demographic condition. As already mentioned, there is a socially acceptable upper limit for the activity ratio. If we take this as fixed, we can substitute in the right-hand side of (6.4) the growth factor for the population of working age, Λ^{dem*}:

$$\Lambda_D^* > \Lambda^{dem*} \qquad (6.5)$$

From a given initial state, the duration of the extensive period depends, on the one hand, on demographic growth, and on the other hand, on the speed and technical character of the expansion. Let us not forget that Γ^* and Φ are synthetic indices summarizing highly complex social processes. In our model Γ^* is dependent on all the real parameters. The extensive period ends sooner if, with other conditions unchanged, the initial wage rate ω_N is lower, or if Φ is closer to 1, that is, the release of labour is slower, and so on. The economic magnitudes that the model treats as exogenous parameters are in fact dependent on economic policy, on the contents of plans and on investment decisions. If, however, condition (6.4)–(6.5) is satisfied, it is inevitable that the system will eventually arrive at full employment.

Formulae (6.3)–(6.5) are very simple and their content might seem trivial: if labour demand increases faster than population, every available person will eventually take up work. And yet these formulae have an important message to convey, which is not self-evident for many present-day macroeconomists. These formulae focus our attention by *selecting* from the various factors that could explain employment and also by *disregarding* certain factors.

The formulae mentioned above direct attention to *long-term* processes. They do not deal with factors that only transiently affect the labour market, but instead they *lay stress on the historical process of creating jobs.* Profound social changes lie behind this process: industrialization, the flow of population from village districts to towns, urbanization, and so on. If this social transformation and the associated economic growth proceed at an appropriate rate, the population will gradually be mobilized even if there are market fluctuations along the way. In the light of this, though it may often seem important, the instantaneous demand for labour only has secondary importance.

In the model the real wage fund depends on employment. But there is no inverse relationship, so that the macro-level labour supply does not depend on real wages. This presents a problem as far as the intensive period is concerned but we shall consider that later. In my opinion, however, one is fully justified in disregarding the above-mentioned inverse relationship in modelling growth during the extensive period. And our model – in the form described so far – has just that aim, namely to formulate a representation of the extensive period. The flow of labour into the firms' (and into the non-profit institutions') sector does not basically depend on wage offers, but rather on job opportunities. *The short-term supply of labour during the extensive period depends effectively on the demand for labour.*

The preceding train of thought is particularly worth the attention of those dealing with macroeconomic problems in less advanced countries: those of Central and Southern Europe, Asia, Africa and Latin America. However important for them the problems that occupy today's professional literature in the advanced capitalist countries (inflation, balance of payments, foreign exchange rate, etc.) may be, it would be a serious error only to be concerned about them. The fundamental questions of employment are ultimately decided by the type of growth process that takes place in the country.

Some data can be provided to illustrate my remarks. Table B.7 of Appendix B draws a comparison between the activity rates in a few European socialist and capitalist countries. The capitalist countries listed are those which, after the Second World War, were at about the same development level as the Eastern-European countries included in the table. Although there is quite a wide variance, the difference between the averages of the two groups is striking. In the capitalist countries the activity rate was about 35–40 per cent in 1975, while it was about 50 per cent in the socialist countries.

And now we can return to the main subject of this chapter, efficiency. *In mobilizing labour as the most important resource of society, in systematically bringing labour into the production process the socialist economy proves to be highly efficient.* This is one of its most important historical achievements.

One-sided or distorted value-judgements are readily found among both adherents and opponents of the socialist system. Either they stress only those factors that improve efficiency in the system, or only those that reduce it. The truth, however, is more complicated than that.

The *same* economic growth pattern and, correspondingly, the same control mechanism which introduce and constantly reproduce shortage on the market of *goods*, will at the same time bring about the absorption of the initially inactive reserves of labour, create full enployment, and then introduce and constantly reproduce shortage on the *labour* market. The *same* growth pattern and control mechanism which inhibit the improvement of *internal* efficiency, that is, improvements in the input–output ratio for resources already drawn into the production, will improve *external* efficiency by activating the previously inactive resources.

The intensive period: full employment, labour shortage

For the moment we shall set aside the problems of transition from the extensive to the intensive period and proceed directly to examine the growth pattern that characterizes an economy in which labour reserves have long been exhausted. It will be useful to explain this first, to make it easier later on to understand certain aspects of the transition.

The most important property of the 'mature' intensive period it that *labour shortage has become chronic.* To avoid misunderstanding: I do not assert that in the intensive period the ability of everyone employed is fully utilized at his job. On pp. 95–102 I tried to explain that the various shortage phenomena (including labour shortage) are among the reasons why the utilization of resources already 'contracted' or 'bought' in the factory is unfavourable. There are machines at a standstill, frozen stocks of goods and idle workers waiting for work, material or machines. What we call labour shortage arises when the firm would be willing to offer labour contracts to more people than are willing to accept them. 'Unemployment on the job', or, an unfavourable labour/output ratio within the firm are not only compatible with labour shortage but mutually reinforce each other.

All our general discussion of the firm in relation to *goods* can now be repeated for the intensive period in relation to *labour.* We know that the firm is in general hardly sensitive at all to input prices. Now, in the intensive period this situation also holds for labour inputs, with the firm hardly sensitive to wages at all. Its demand for labour would not be reduced by a general wage increase, nor by a change in the proportions of wages and the prices of materials and machinery, to the advantage of the former.

Shortage induces the firm to hoard input stocks, and this too has its equivalent in labour: labour hoarding. The firm will not send away a worker who has become unecessary even if the latter could easily find a job elsewhere. The firm's standpoint is that its demand for labour will surely grow in the future and it might then be difficult to find the required workers.

After noting these points, let us again consider the growth model. In the original form set out in Chapter 3 it served to represent the extensive period. What is the minimum transformation that would render the model usable for an examination of the intensive period?

The employment equation (3.23) must be replaced by two others: equations (6.6) and (6.7). One of these is the equation for labour supply:

$$L_S(t) = L_{S,I} \Lambda_{S,I}^t, \qquad (6.6)$$

in which $L_S(t)$ is *labour supply* in year t, $L_{S,I}$ is labour supply in the initial year of the intensive period, and $\Lambda_{S,I}$ is the growth factor for labour supply. This may be less than 1 but it could also be larger. In Hungary, for example, labour supply measured in terms of the number of available workers is tending to stagnate, though in terms of hours worked it shows a slight downward tendency, which will probably continue in the future, since working hours are being reduced by law over an increasing proportion of the economy.

In reality, during the intensive period macro-level labour supply may be influenced by changes in nominal or real wages. For example, the mother of a young child compares the salary she could get for working for a firm with the amount the state grants to mothers who care for their children at home; but even in such decisions the limited capacity of nurseries and kindergartens, family circumstances, etc., may be more weighty arguments. For this reason, the effect of the causal linkage from wage $\rightarrow$ labour supply seems rather weak.

A few representatives of the 'disequilibrium theory' have put forward the idea that there is a connection between excess demand on the market for consumer goods, and labour supply. Thus it would not be worth the effort of earning a lot of money if one was unable to spend it. Our own experience does not support the existence of such a relationship, however. Household forced savings caused by shortage would have to arise at extreme levels in order to deter a large number of people from taking up wage-earning jobs.

I would not reject outright the idea of including in the model – at a later stage of the research, particularly if the model is already applied to econometric analysis – one or two additional endogenous interrelations between wages and labour supply, and/or between shortage and labour supply. For the time being, however, in this first theoretical approximation, this does not seem justified. The description based on (6.6) – in which labour supply is a function of time alone – seems appropriate as a first provisional approximation.

The new form of the *employment* equation, in accordance with the definition of the intensive period, is the following:

$$N(t) = L_S(t). \qquad (6.7)$$

This equation is numbered (A.10-int) in Appendix A. In comparing equations (A.10-ext) and (A.10-int) we can see that in our model the 'short-side rule'[5] prevails in the long run. While demand is relatively low, equation (A.10-ext) is valid; since supply later lags behind the demand for labour, equation (A.10-int) becomes valid. This dichotomy can be summed up as follows:

$$N(t) = \min(L_D(t), L_S(t)). \tag{6.8}$$

The 'disequilibrium theory' likes to use formulae of this kind when demand and supply alternately prove to be the short side, and the situation may suddenly switch over from excess demand to excess supply, or from excess supply to excess demand. This does not apply in our case. *The process in question is irreversible.* After several decades of a demand-constrained labour market, it switches over into a resource-constrained situation – but from there it cannot return to its former state. As long as ownership and other institutional arrangements of the system remain unchanged, chronic labour shortage will continue to characterize the system. Therefore, it would be useless[6] to build the 'switching rule' (6.8) into the present model.

---

[5] We would be more consistent with the spirit of our model if we did not use the 'short-side rule' at this point, either. The truth is, as I have mentioned, that partial labour shortage existed in certain sectors or in certain geographical regions even in the period of large labour reserves. And, in the period of labour shortage, there still exists a certain amount of external reserve labour which could be drawn into production by creating favourable employment opportunities, perhaps by better labour conditions, a service apartment, or better salaries. It would not be particularly difficult to model labour shortage and slack simultaneously, as we succeeded in doing in this model for the goods market.

[6] What is more, its mathematical treatment within a difference equation system is also inconvenient.

A further change to be effected in the model is the completion of equation (A.11), explaining general shortage, by adding the following feedback term:

$$+ \zeta_L (L_D(t) - L_S(t) - \Lambda_{S,I}^t Z_{L,I}^*), \qquad (6.9)$$

in which $Z_{L,I}^*$ is the *initial value of normal labour shortage* at the beginning of the intensive period. The product $\Lambda_{S,I}^t Z_{L,I}^*$ is normal labour shortage in year t. Both factors in the product are specified as exogenous parameters. The introduction of this new factor in the equation reveals that if *labour* shortage is more intensive than normal, this will intensify *general* shortage, and conversely.

Let us call the original model as summarized in Appendix A, but with the employment interrelations modified according to (6.6) and (6.7), and with the shortage equation augmented by the term (6.9), *the model of the intensive period. All the qualitative propositions and conjectures about the model of the extensive period, set out in Chapters 4 and 5, also hold,* mutatis mutandis, *in respect of the model of the intensive period.* The real conditions for the system to be able to grow can be given, and a feasible normal path exists. The system is controllable. Concerning its stability everything said on pp. 81–8 could be repeated. In order to avoid repetition, however, we shall not go into details. We merely add a few remarks about the normal path.

In respect of the extensive period we explained that along the normal path, interrelation (4.6) is valid: $\Gamma^* = \Lambda_N^* \Psi$. Since employment is now determined by the supply side, an alternative relationship holds for the intensive period:

$$\Gamma^* = \Lambda_{S,I} \Psi. \qquad (6.10)$$

This is the well-known Harrod–Domar relationship, reformulated in the language of our model. On the left-hand side we have the growth factor corresponding to the 'warranted' growth rate, and on the right-hand side, that corresponding to the 'natural' growth rate. On the left-hand side, the general growth factor is jointly determined by the set of real parameters in the model, and on the right-hand side is the product of labour supply and the growth factor for the (vintage) productivity.

When conditions (A), (B) and (C), as specified at (4.3), are satisfied the economic system also has an H–N normal path in the intensive period. Taking into consideration the long-term trends, there exists a growth path along which the reproducible stock and flow variables (production, investment, stocks, consumption) increase at a constant and uniform rate even during the intensive period. On the same path normal shortage intensity (measured in the original units, $\bar{Z}$) is constant.

The normal H–N path is incompatible with possible economic policy efforts to accelerate growth beyond the 'natural rate'. This could be achieved only if the accumulation ratio grew continuously over time, with the real wage rate growing more slowly than productivity, and if the conditions set out as (4.3) are violated in other respects as well. This type of growth could be examined theoretically, but this would lead us away from the family of H–N models to which the model presented in this book also belongs. Therefore, I must be satisfied merely to indicate the problem, and cannot undertake a proper examination of it here.

Growth rates in the extensive and intensive periods

At the end of the preceding section we only dealt with *qualitative* analysis. It turned out that the models for the two periods have identical general 'system-theoretical' properties. Such properties include the ability to grow, and the existence of a feasible normal path with its exponentially growing character, controllability, stability, etc. But now we shall examine a few of the *quantitative* differences between the two periods.

With the aid of our model we shall compare the conditions of extensive and intensive growth in Hungary as if in a laboratory. Thus we shall disregard all other external and internal conditions, and we shall not deal with the specific difficulties of the transition from one period to the next. In Figure 17 we show the *accumulation ratio* along the normal path on the horizontal axis.

$$i(t) = [B(t) + \Delta U(t) + \Delta V(t)]/(1 - \alpha) X(t). \quad (6.11)$$

Along the normal H–N path the accumulation ratio is constant: $i(t) = i^*$ for every t. On the vertical axis the normal growth rate is shown, denoted by r^*: $r^* = (\Gamma^* - 1)$.

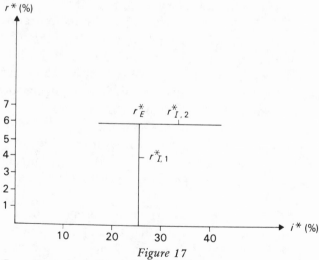

Figure 17

Growth rate in the intensive period and the accumulation ratio

The point r_E^* is the normal growth rate for the *extensive* period. This is based on the computations already carried out in the simulations reported earlier. The *intensive* period is represented by two points: two hypothetical 'pure cases'. (Of course, there may be transitional cases between the two.) Both points indicate a pair (i^*, r^*) associated with a potential normal path H–N.

In determining the left-hand point $r_{I,1}^*$, it is stipulated that the system should grow with the same accumulation ratio in the intensive period as in the extensive one. In that case the growth rate of the economy is considerably lower: instead of the 6 per cent characteristic of the extensive period it falls to about 4 per cent.

The determination of the right-hand point $r_{I,2}^*$ is based on the assumption that economic policymakers wish to maintain the normal growth rate of the extensive period at all costs. With this in mind, it is prepared to raise the accumulation ratio, or, equivalently to depress the consumption ratio. To achieve that, the initial wage rate $\omega_{N,I}$ for the intensive period must be considerably below what it would be in the case of a lower accumulation ratio. In order to keep up the rate of growth, the accumulation ratio must be significantly increased as compared with the extensive period. The growth rate typical of the extensive period can be maintained – even without changing other conditions – but only at the expense of consumption.

In reality, along with the exhaustion of reserves of labour there are also other difficulties that impede growth in several Eastern-European socialist countries, including Hungary. We shall point out three of these:

(1) The shift in world market price proportions shifted the terms of trade to the disadvantage of these countries. It is particularly the rising relative price of energy that gives cause for concern.

(2) The recession in the advanced capitalist countries and, in general, the slow-down in the growth of the world economy accompanied by protectionist measures render exports more difficult.

(3) In earlier decades the development of infrastructural sectors was neglected. Some acceleration of development in certain sectors (for example, in housing, road construction, etc.) can hardly be postponed any further. And development in these fields is particularly investment-intensive.

These phenomena are frequently discussed both by academic economists and by economic managers in Eastern Europe. The train of thought developed in this book was merely intended to support the widely accepted view according to which *the exhaustion of labour reserves is sufficient in itself to force the economic system to leave its old growth path for a new and much slower one.*

Transition from the extensive to the intensive period: choice of technique

The switch-over to the new growth path takes place with some difficulty. I believe that our model accentuates one of the characteristic features of the real economic system when it focuses attention on routine behaviour, repetition, and the reproduction of an earlier *status quo*. In talking about norms on pp. 77–81 I emphasized the important role of habit in fixing norms. Shocks to the system, or thorough-going and persistent changes, do compel the norms to change, yet this does not take place overnight.

For example, let us take the attitudes to do with *choice of technique*. During the extensive period two kinds of tendency made themselves felt. The first is connected with the expansion drive. Since investment resources are limited, while labour is available in effectively unlimited amounts, the pressure for the fastest possible rate of expansion orientates firms towards choosing relatively less investment-intensive and more labour-intensive techniques. The same factor motivates them not to scrap old and out-dated machinery and not to demolish dilapidated buildings, but to maintain them and build new plants beside them. The second tendency has exactly the opposite effect: engineers and other specialists in the factories are drawn towards the latest techniques. Installing these involves less difficulty and the results are easier and more pleasant to operate. To a certain extent, 'professional pride' also encourages rapid modernization. The attraction of the new techniques is felt, not only in the factories themselves, but also by upper-level economic managers and politicians.

Finally, as a macro-average, a compromise between the two tendencies is asserted. There is no question of a deliberately chosen 'optimum combination', but some mixture comes about rather accidentally. It often happens that in the same enterprise both backward and up-to-date sections function in parallel. This is one reason why the dispersion in the 'degree of modernization' can be so wide within one and the same country.

In the literature it has more than once been suggested that the role neoclassical theory assigns to the interest rate – and, in general, to the prices of production factors – in rational investment decisions can evolve best in a socialist economy. I do not wish to comment on this view from the standpoint of *normative* theory. However, approaching it from the standpoint of a *descriptive* theory of socialist practice, I can say that such calculations do not materially influence the choice of technique.[7]

---

[7] This is an important argument, showing that it was justified to disregard the rate of interest, nominal wages, as well as monetary and fiscal variables in the macro-modelling of the control of investment.

We can advance a proposition of a more general character: *there is no clear and well-defined signal system and calculation principle to orientate the choice of technique during the extensive period of the socialist economy.* Consequently, the reality of the extension period is appropriately reflected by our model, in that it does not include any endogenous control over choice of technique, but instead describes technical progress simply as a function of time.

As the extensive period comes to an end, the perception of partial labour shortage becomes more frequent. And later it becomes apparent to almost anyone that the economy's labour reserves are exhausted. The concrete manifestations of labour shortage, and the problems they cause, serve as a *signal system* stimulating an accelerated introduction of labour-saving techniques.

A considerable time passes from the initial perceptions of shortage to its general *recognition*, and from recognition to new *decisions* about choice of technique; this in turn only slowly has its *effect* in terms of releasing labour. The investment vintage that was started, say, in the first year of the intensive period will lead to the operation of production capacity only G years later. Even if this new vintage already embodies the technique that is the most labour-saving, it will only represent a small fraction of the fixed capital of the period. This is all the more true since in the intensive period the rate of scrapping hardly accelerates. Quantity drive persists and firms 'haven't the heart' to discard old machinery, which does, after all, produce something.

The dynamics of the transition are illustrated, schematically in Figure 18.

During the extensive period decision-makers only receive quantity signals relating to the shortage of investment resources ('capital shortage'), and not to labour,

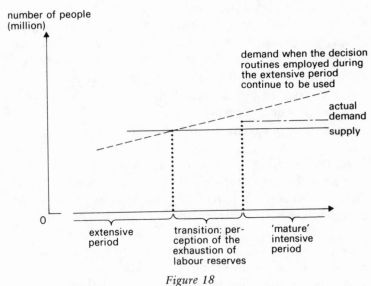

Figure 18
Dynamics of the transition from the extensive to the intensive period

generally. (Apart from those sectors or districts already experiencing a partial labour shortage.) As opposed to this, in the 'mature' intensive period, when the economy has become accustomed to normal labour shortage, quantity signals are received equally and simultaneously relating both to labour shortage *and* to investment resource shortage, and these orientate the decision-makers in their choice of technique. It may well be possible to build such a signal system, with its associated feedbacks and controls endogenously into the model. This is one of the tasks that awaits further research.

So far we have only discussed the shift in attitudes towards the choice of technique. Actually, the adjustment is much more comprehensive. *All norms have to adjust to accommodate the new situation*, but this will not take place without resistance. *It is particularly in regard to the most important norms, that is, the growth factors* Γ_j, *that adjustment takes place with difficulty. Past expectations, hopes and illusions about the growth rate persist.*

At this point, the sphere of problems discussed on pp. 81–8, to do with the mathematical stability of growth models comes closer to real life. During the transition from the extensive to the intensive period the system is unstable. Since the real parameters have changed, the earlier norms and control mechanisms are *no longer* able to drive the system back to its old normal path. On the other hand, the new norms and control mechanisms have *not yet* been established. In a computer simulation, or in theoretical analysis, it is easy to modify a model of the economic system to shift over to the intensive path. Real economic systems, however, can only adjust themselves to new conditions accompanied by friction, fluctuations and often with much pain.

7

Closing Remarks

Nothing discussed in this short book can be regarded as a *final* report on an accomplished research project; it is more in the nature of a progress report. I already stressed when introducing the model that the principal result of the work completed so far is the model itself, and I have tried to give the reader a feel for how the apparatus could be used for studying economic problems. There is quite a number of questions which we shall examine using the *present* model. This work can be done either analytically, or by computer simulation. It is particularly important to strengthen the empirical background and make some attempt to verify the model by macroeconometric analysis.

The study of a system growing at a constant and uniform rate is of great theoretical and practical importance. It will, however, be worth taking a step forward and searching for a formulation more suited to describe growth *at a variable rate*, either decelerating or accelerating, or growth *at a variable rate* with different rates for each sector or each type of process. This is a question of underlying assumptions. In particular, it would be desirable to relax the most drastic simplifications: the exclusion of substitution, and the exogenous treatment of technical progress.

Many important aspects of the functioning of a socialist economy can be described with the formulation used here, based on techniques borrowed from mathematical control theory, the idea of control according to norms, and so on. Yet many important features are necessarily omitted from the description, as a consequence of the limitations of our approach. There surely does not exist some other perfect model. It seems rather more important to construct a series of different models – each of them being deficient and one-sided in some way, but mutually complementary – if we want to elaborate a more complete and more comprehensive macrodynamic theory of the socialist economy.

By pointing out the research tasks that still face us I wanted to make clear that the reader cannot be less satisfied with the model and more impatient for further progress than the author himself. It would be easy for my critics to try to convince me that one or other variable should be included in the model, or that the structure of certain equations should be modified. These are questions of secondary importance in the model. What I want to insist on – if I may use the word – are the *essential* properties of the model, that is, its *specific character*. Having reached the end of the study, let me point out a few of these specific features.

The role of shortage

One of the most characteristic features of the model is its treatment of shortage. As I mentioned on pp. 17–18 it is increasingly recognized in econometrics, sociometrics and psychometrics that there exist variables that may not be measurable directly but still play an important role in explanatory and causal theories. With a few exceptions,[1]

---

[1] First of all the pioneering books of I. Adelman and C. T. Morris must be mentioned: *Society, Politics and Economic Development: A Quantitative Approach*, Johns Hopkins Press, Baltimore, 1976;

however, this recognition is not reflected in the construction of formal growth models. In this respect the introduction of the variable Z into the model represents a novel departure in the growth theory literature. To me this procedure seemed to be both tractable and a useful step forward.

What I consider most important in this respect is not whether we accept the actual statistical methodology of the first experimental computations to determine the variable Z, nor whether we agree with the specific structure of equation (A.11) explaining changes in shortage, or with the form in which Z appears in other equations. All such details can be modified and improved. The key point is the methodological conception itself, *whereby we may introduce into macro-models and growth models, as appropriate, unconventional latent variables for the description and explanation of complex phenomena, even if it might not be possible to observe and measure them directly*. This is a principle which may be worth considering in modelling other kinds of system too.

Aside from the *methodological* lesson, the introduction of the variable Z can also teach us something about the structure of growth models. In the mathematical economics literature two subject areas can easily be distinguished. On the one hand, short-term macromodels feature such problems as full employment and unemployment, potential and less than potential output, aggregate excess demand and aggregate excess supply, and so on. On the other hand, dynamic growth models investigate questions of the growth rate, investment, technical progress and labour productivity. The present model is a modest attempt to combine these two subject areas. Although it uses fixed coefficients in the mathematical sense, as far

---

and *Economic Growth and Social Equity in Developing Countries*, Stanford University Press, Stanford, 1973.

as the economic content is concerned, we specify *input functions*, and in such a way that *the efficiency of production and investment depends on the macro-state of the market, its distance from the Walrasian state, that is, on the intensity of shortage*. We sought to demonstrate that *the macro-state of the market (in our case shortage), the efficiency of input utilization, and the overall growth rate are interdependent*. I may be excessively optimistic, but I feel that the model is rather richer in this respect than has been demonstrated by the analysis thus far. Much more can be 'extracted' from it in the course of further research.

The immanent regularities of a socialist economy

Finally, in my own judgement, the most important property of the model is the way in which it describes the socialist economy. Many tend towards the view that the socialist economy should be interpreted as a specific form of 'administrative organization'. On this view, what happens in the system depends on economic management. Although certain physical and technological conditions are given, decisions are otherwise unconstrained.

The philosophy of the present model differs from this. The operation of the economic systems of the Eastern-European socialist countries reveals some characteristic regularities.[2] At each level of decision-making *the behaviour of the decision-maker is in a certain sense*

---

[2] It would be too pretentious to call these regularities 'laws'. A stricter logical analysis and, primarily, more thorough empirical observation over a much longer period would be necessary to find out which of the regularities formulated earlier should be regarded as a 'law of motion'.

'regular': definite impulses and signals lead to definite consequences.[3]

This does not mean that decision-makers are lifeless screws in a piece of machinery. I have not the slightest intention of denying that decision-makers have a choice and, at the same time, responsibility. Economic policy and planning operate on an economy-wide basis and exert extremely strong social effects.

That is why two different approaches are necessary in economics: the normative and the descriptive. Normative models have a say in economic policy and in the determination of national economic plans *before* definite decisions are made. They help to reveal the alternatives for choice and to forecast the consequences of decisions. On the other hand, for the descriptive–explanatory theory a series of *past* decisions is already available: by analysing these, it tries to discover whether they exhibit any common regularities.

What our model has to offer in this respect is not satisfactory. I would be happy to see a better description. What is really important is actually to undertake the task of describing, with a formalized theoretical model, the internal regularities in the growth of a socialist economy and in the control of this growth.

---

[3] It is only for the sake of simplifying the mathematical formalization that this is represented by single-valued and deterministic relationships. In fact, stochastic regularities are involved.

Appendix A
Summary of the Model

NOTATION

Variables

---

t = time, integer variable (interpretation: serial number of the year)

θ = time-shift, integer variable

τ = time-shift, integer variable

A = current input

B = investment input

H = household purchases

J = number of jobs created by the investment vintage

K = investment commitment

L_D = labour demand

L_S = labour supply

M = volume of the investment vintage

N = employment

p = standard productivity

q = vintage productivity

U = output stock

V = input stock

W = real wage fund

X = production

Y = firms' purchases

Z = shortage (the macroindex of shortage)

Real Parameters

Symbol	C = coefficient G = growth factor	Equation number	Interpretation
G	—	(A.3), (A.5), (A.8), (A.9)	gestation period
$L_{S,I}$	—	(A.10-int)	labour supply in the initial year of the intensive period
T	—	(A.8), (A.9)	economic life of fixed capital
Z_0^*	—	(A.26)	normal shortage in the initial year
Z_L^*	—	(A.10-int)	normal labour shortage
α_X	C	(A.4)	current input coefficient
α_Z	C	(A.4)	real effect of shortage on current inputs
β_M	C	(A.3), (A.5)	expenditure share of the investment vintage
β_Z	C	(A.5)	real effect of shortage on investment inputs
Γ_Z	G	(A.26)	growth factor for the shortage macroindex
ζ_K	C	(A.11)	effect of investment commitment on shortage
ζ_U	C	(A.11)	effect of output stocks on shortage
ζ_V	C	(A.11)	effect of input stocks on shortage
ζ_Z	C	(A.11)	autoregressive effect of shortage
ζ_L	C	(A.11-int)	effect of labour shortage on shortage
χ	C	(A.6)	initial job-creation coefficient
λ	C	(A.7)	initial vintage productivity coefficient

Symbol	C = coefficient G = growth factor	Equation number	Interpretation
$\Lambda_{S,I}$	G	(A.11-int)	growth factor for labour supply in the intensive period
π_Z	C	(A.8)	real effect of shortage on standard productivity
Φ	G	(A.6)	growth factor of job creation
Ψ	G	(A.7)	growth factor for vintage productivity

Control Parameters

Symbol	C = coefficient G = growth factor	Equation number	Interpretation
M_0	—	(A.17)	normal volume of investment vintage in the initial year
Γ_H	G	(A.25)	normal growth factor for consumption
Γ_K	G	(A.24)	normal growth factor for investment commitment
Γ_M	G	(A.17)	normal growth factor for the volume of investment vintage
Γ_Y	G	(A.19)	normal growth factor for firms' purchases
η_V	C	(A.14)	feedback from input stocks to the firms' purchasing decisions
η_Z	C	(A.14)	feedback from shortage to the firms' purchasing decisions
μ_H	C	(A.12)	feedback from consumption to the decision on the volume of the investment vintage

Symbol	C = coefficient G = Growth factor	Equation number	Interpretation
μ_K	C	(A.12)	feedback from investment commitment to the decision on the volume of the investment vintage
μ_Z	C	(A.12)	feedback from shortage to the decision on the volume of the investment vintage
ξ_U	C	(A.13)	feedback from output stocks to the decision on production
ξ_Z	C	(A.13)	feedback from shortage to the decision on production
ρ	C	(A.22)	normal output stock coefficient
σ	C	(A.23)	normal input stock coefficient
χ_W	C	(A.20)	spending ratio
χ_Z	C	(A.20)	feedback from shortage to the households' purchasing decisions
ω_H	C	(A.16)	feedback from consumption to the real wage fund
ω_N	C	(A.21)	initial real wage rate
Ω	G	(A.21)	normal growth factor for the real wage rate

EQUATIONS

Real Sphere

Stock equations

Output stock

$$U(t) = U(t-1) + X(t-1) - Y(t-1) - H(t-1). \quad (A.1)$$

Input stock

$$V(t) = V(t-1) + Y(t-1) - A(t-1) - B(t-1). \quad (A.2)$$

Investment commitment

$$K(t) = \sum_{\theta=1}^{G-1} \sum_{\tau=\theta+1}^{G} \beta_M(\tau) M(t-\theta). \quad (A.3)$$

Input-output relations

Current input

$$A(t) = \alpha_X X(t) + \alpha_Z (Z(t) - Z^*(t)). \quad (A.4)$$

Investment input

$$B(t) = \sum_{\theta=0}^{G-1} \beta_M(\theta+1) M(t-\theta) + \beta_Z(Z(t) - Z^*(t)). \quad (A.5)$$

Job creation of the investment vintage

$$J(t) = \chi \Phi^t M(t). \quad (A.6)$$

Vintage productivity

$$q(t) = \lambda \Psi^t. \quad (A.7)$$

Standard productivity

$$p(t) = \sum_{\theta=G}^{T+G-1} J(t-\theta) q(t-\theta) \Big/ \sum_{\theta=G}^{T+G-1} J(t-\theta)$$
$$- (\Psi^t / \Gamma_Z^t) \pi_Z (Z(t) - Z^*(t)). \quad (A.8)$$

Labour demand

$$L_D(t) = \sum_{\theta = G}^{T+G-1} J(t - \theta). \qquad \text{(A.9)}$$

Labour supply (only in the intensive period)

$$L_S(t) = \Lambda_{S,I}^t L_{S,I}. \qquad \text{(A.9-int)}$$

Employment

$$N(t) = L_D(t). \qquad \text{(A.10-ext)}$$

$$N(t) = L_S(t). \qquad \text{(A.10-int)}$$

Shortage

$$\begin{aligned}
Z(t) = {}& Z^*(t) + \zeta_K(K(t) - K^*(t)) \\
& - \zeta_U(U(t) - U^*(t)) \\
& - \zeta_V(V(t) - V^*(t)) \qquad \text{(A.11)} \\
& + \zeta_Z(Z(t-1) - Z^*(t-1)) \\
& + \zeta_L(L_D(t) - L_S(t) - \Lambda_{S,I}^t Z_{L,I}^*).
\end{aligned}$$

(*Remark*: the last term on the right hand side
only figures in the model of the intensive period)

Control Sphere

Control equations

Volume of the investment vintage

$$\begin{aligned}
M(t) - M^*(t) = {}& \mu_H(H(t-1) - H_{\text{plan}}^*(t-1)) \\
& - \mu_K(K(t) - K^*(t)) \qquad \text{(A.12)} \\
& - \mu_Z(Z(t) - Z^*(t)).
\end{aligned}$$

Production

$$X(t) - X^*(t) = -\xi_U(U(t) - U^*(t)) + \xi_Z(Z(t) - Z^*(t)). \quad \text{(A.13)}$$

Firms' purchases

$$Y(t) - Y^*(t) = -\eta_V(V(t) - V^*(t)) - \eta_Z(Z(t) - Z^*(t)). \quad \text{(A.14)}$$

Household purchases

$$H(t) - H_h^*(t) = -\chi_Z(Z(t) - Z^*(t)). \quad \text{(A.15)}$$

Real wage fund

$$W(t) - W^*(t) = -\omega_H(H(t-1) - H_{\text{plan}}^*(t-1)). \quad \text{(A.16)}$$

Normal values of the control variables

Normal volume of the investment vintage

$$M^*(t) = \Gamma_M M^*(t-1) = \Gamma_M^t M_0. \quad \text{(A.17)}$$

Normal production

$$X^*(t) = p(t) N(t). \quad \text{(A.18)}$$

Firms' normal purchases

$$Y^*(t) = \Gamma_Y Y(t-1). \quad \text{(A.19)}$$

Normal household purchases (derived from real wages)

$$H_h^*(t) = \chi_W W(t). \quad \text{(A.20)}$$

Normal real wage fund

$$W^*(t) = \omega_N \Omega^t N(t). \qquad (A.21)$$

Normal value of signals acting as feedback

Normal output stock

$$U^*(t) = \rho(H(t-1) + Y(t-1)). \qquad (A.22)$$

Normal input stock

$$V^*(t) = \sigma(A(t-1) + B(t-1)). \qquad (A.23)$$

Normal investment commitment

$$K^*(t) = \Gamma_K K(t-1). \qquad (A.24)$$

Normal consumption

$$H^*_{\text{plan}}(t) = \Gamma_H H(t-1). \qquad (A.25)$$

Normal shortage

$$Z^*(t) = \Gamma_Z Z^*(t-1) = \Gamma_Z^t Z_0^*. \qquad (A.26)$$

Appendix B
Statistical Tables

Table B.1   Partial indicators (Hungarian data)

	(1) *Orders refused by constructing industry (orders refused divided by annual output, percentage)*	(2) *Queuing for cars (backlog of unfilled orders divided by annual sales: queuing time in years)*
1965		3.34
1966		0.69
1967		0.89
1968		1.66
1969		3.75
1970	49.8	2.95
1971	24.9	2.65
1972	9.2	2.16
1973	7.5	1.28
1974	17.0	0.57
1975	30.3	2.00
1976	39.4	2.85
1977	41.0	4.18
1978	26.5	5.48
1979	17.0	3.77

Sources: Column (1) Ministry of Construction and Urban Development; Column (2) Enterprise 'Merkur' (in charge of selling cars).

Table B.2   Construction periods in Hungary and Japan

Hungarian data: average construction time	1976	32.5 months
(the sample covers several industries)	1977	32.3 months
Japanese data: average construction time	1966	
wood industry		12 months
synthetics		16 months
pharmaceuticals		6 months
textiles		12 months
power stations		30 months

Source: Z. Pacsi, 'Á megvalósitási idő alakulása és szerepe a beruházásokban' [Construction periods of investment projects], *Pénzügyi Szemle*, **23** (1979), 137–59.

Table B.3   Investment (international comparion) – annual growth rates (percentages)

Country	1968–72	1973–77
Bulgaria	5.9	9.7
GDR	7.2	6.1
Hungary	8.0	8.5
Poland	13.3	10.5
Austria	7.5	2.5
Denmark	7.0	2.0
Finland	10.9	0.6
Greece	7.7	−3.5
Ireland	6.7	5.6
Italy	6.0	4.1
Spain	9.9	0.4

Sources: For capitalist countries, UN and OECD data; for socialist countries, national statistical yearbooks.

Table B.4 Composition of stocks (international comparison)

Country and date		Share of output stocks in total stocks (percentages)
GDR	1963	15.4
Hungary	1976	11.9
Poland	1975	17.0
Austria	1976	32.1
Canada	1970	31.3
Japan	1975	53.2
Sweden	1977	38.2

Source: A. Chikán and M. Nagy, 'Adelékok a készletnövekedés és készletstruktura kapcsolatának kérdéséhez' [Data concerning the relationship between growth and the structure of stocks], manuscript, Budapest, 1979.

Table B.5 Stock coefficients (international comparison) – stocks per unit of manufacturing production

Country	1970	1975	1976
Hungary	0.808	0.829	0.850
Canada	0.433	0.428	
Great Britain	0.483	0.441	
Japan	0.361	0.331	
Sweden			0.394
USA	0.339		

Sources: as Table B.4.

Appendix B

Table B.6   Utilization of fixed capital (international comparison) –
actual consumption of electric energy as a percentage of the nominal
maximal consumption

Country	1966	1967	1968
Hungary	14.9	15.7	15.2
Great Britain	18.8	18.2	18.9
South Korea	18.5	19.8	23.5

Source: J. Rimler, 'Multbeli trendek és jövőbeli tendenciák a magyar feldolgo-
zóipar állóeszközeinek kihasználásában [Past trends and future tendencies in
the utilization of fixed capital in Hungarian manufacturing], mimeographed.
MTA Közgazdaságtudományi Intézete, Budapest, 1979.

Table B.7   Activity rates (international comparison)

Country	Activity rate in 1975 (percentages)
Bulgaria	53.4
Czechoslovakia	50.1
Hungary	49.6
Rumania	55.9
Greece	42.3
Ireland	38.0
Italy	37.3
Portugal	39.0
Spain	34.9

Source: ILO Statistical Yearbooks.

Appendix C
Illustrative Computation: Estimation of the Shortage Macroindex

We made use of four shortage indicators: for three of them we had a 15-year time-series, and for the remaining one a 10-year time-series. For illustration, we present two of them in Table B.1. The other two are an index of building materials shortage drawn up by János Gács,[1] and the deviation of household savings from its own trend.[2]

Using these data, we carried out a principal component analysis.[3] The first principal component computed using this approach has the important property that it explains the largest proportion of total variance of the observed

---

[1] See J. Gács, 'Hiány és támogatott fejlesztés (Tendenciák az épitőanyagipar irányításának történetében)' [Shortage and subsidized development: tendencies in the history of management of the building industry], *Közgazdasági Szemle*, 23 (1976), 1043–60; and J. Gács, 'Adaptive Planning and the Cyclical Character of Economic Activity', mimeographed, Institute for Market Research, Budapest, 1976.

[2] The latter two partial shortage indicators do not satisfy, in their present form, stipulation (ii) made in Section 3.1: their origins do not correspond to the Walrasian state free from all shortage phenomena.

[3] Peter Wellisch helped me to clarify the mathematical–statistical problems. He also did the computations that serve as a basis for Table C.1.

variables (in our case: the partial shortage indicators). In other words, it measures the combined motion over time of the partial indicators. In this illustrative example the first principal component is therefore regarded as a numerical approximation to the macroindex $\bar{Z}(t)$.

Now we shall summarize what is involved, mathematically, in defining the first principal component.

The partial shortage indicators are standardized into variables with zero mean, and unit variance. The matrix of correlation coefficients is then determined, and the eigenvector associated with the largest eigenvalue of the matrix is computed. The first principal component is that linear combination of the partial (standardized) indicators using the components of the above eigenvector as coefficients.

The results proved to be satisfactory. The macroindex time series $\bar{Z}(t)$ are indicated in Table C.1 and illustrated

Table C.1   The macroindex of shortage (based on Hungarian data)

Year	Index based on 14-year time-series	Index based on 9-year time-series
1965	0.412	—
1966	0.430	—
1967	0.429	—
1968	0.544	—
1969	0.600	—
1970	0.548	0.548
1971	0.498	0.486
1972	0.400	0.404
1973	0.401	0.401
1974	0.456	0.447
1975	0.508	0.496
1976	0.505	0.503
1977	0.553	0.531
1978	0.496	0.479

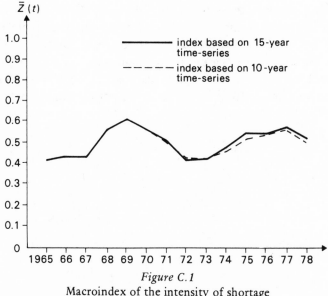

$\bar{Z}(t)$

———— index based on 15-year time-series

– – – – index based on 10-year time-series

Figure C.1
Macroindex of the intensity of shortage

in Figure C.1. If we use only the 14-year time-series, the index $\bar{Z}(t)$ explains 65 per cent of the total variance of the partial indicators. If we are content with the 9-year time-series, but also use the additional time-series available for that period, we are able to explain 66 per cent of the total variance. The fact that the macroindex series obtained by using all four partial indicators closely fits the longer time-series based on only three partial indicators is also reassuring. To explain two-thirds of the variance is about what could be expected on the basis of economic intuition. It points to rather strong positive correlations between the partial indicators while also leaving room for the influence exerted by specific explanatory factors on the different manifestations of shortage.

We hope that the reader will accept the above argument with appropriate caution. We should not over-value the actual computations given in Table C.1. Only a very few partial shortage indicators were used; and, apart from the data, there is uncertainty about the methodology. Although a good case can be made for using principal component analysis, it may be that future research will find a better method for the selection of the function ϕ.

Index